Critical Essays in English and American Literature is a series for both the scholarly and the general reader. Books in the series are published occasionally by the University of Pittsburgh Press.

WILLIAM FAULKNER

An Estimate of his Contribution to the Modern American Novel

by

Mary Cooper Robb

UNIVERSITY OF PITTSBURGH PRESS

PITTSBURGH: 1963

LIBRARY OF CONGRESS CATALOG CARD NUMBER: 57-9063

© 1957 University of Pittsburgh Press
Printed in U.S.A.
Third Printing, 1961
Fourth Printing, 1963

Lithographed in U.S.A. by
EDWARDS BROTHERS, INC.
Ann Arbor, Michigan

WILLIAM FAULKNER

Preface

I feel that this award was not made to me as a man but to my work—a life's work in the agony and sweat of human spirit, not for glory and least of all for profit, but to create out of the materials of the human spirit something which did not exist before. So this award is only mine in trust. It will not be difficult to find a dedication for the money part of it commensurate with the purpose and significance of its origin. But I would like to do the same with the acclaim too, by using this moment as a pinnacle from which I might be listened to by the young men and women already dedicated to the same anguish and travail, among whom is already that one who will some day stand here where I am standing.

Our tragedy today is a general and universal physical fear, so long sustained by now that we can even bear it. There are no longer problems of the spirit. There is only the question: when will I be blown up? Because of this the young man or woman writing today has forgotten the problems of the human heart in conflict with itself which alone can make good writing because only that is worth writing about, worth the agony and the sweat.

He must learn them again. He must teach himself that the basest of all things is to be afraid; and, teaching himself that, forget it forever, leaving no room in his workshop for anything but the old verities and truths of the heart, the old universal truths lacking which any story is ephemeral and doomed—love and honor and pity and pride and compassion and sacrifice. Until he does so he labors under a curse. He writes not of love but of lust, of defeats in which nobody loses anything of value, of victories without hope and worst of all without pity or compassion. His griefs grieve on no universal bones, leaving no scars. He writes not of the heart but of the glands.

Until he relearns these things he will write as though he stood among and watched the end of man. I decline to accept the end of man. It is easy enough to say that man is immortal simply because he will endure; that when the last ding-dong of doom has clanged and faded from the last worthless rock hanging tideless in the last red and dying evening, that even then there will still be one more sound: that of his puny inexhaustible voice, still talking. I refuse to accept this. I believe that man will not merely endure: he will prevail. He is immortal, not because he alone among creatures has an inexhaustible voice, but because he has a soul, a spirit capable of compassion and sacrifice and endurance. The poet's, the writer's duty is to write about these things. It is his privilege to help man endure by lifting his heart, by reminding him of the courage and honor and hope and pride and compassion and pity and sacrifice which have been the glory of his past. The poet's voice need not merely be the record of man, it can be one of the props, the pillars to help him endure and prevail.[1]

These are the words with which William Faulkner accepted the 1950 Nobel prize for literature, awarded to him for his "powerful and artistically independent contribution to the new American novel."[2] They express the ideas, the artistic creed, of an author whom critics regard as one of the important figures in modern fiction. For that reason Faulkner's statement must be considered in any discussion of his work. If, as Bernard De Voto says, no novelist has more than one story to tell,[3] it should be possible to discover in Faulkner's novels and short stories the assertion of a consistent view of life and some constants of expression. And that same assertion should be the one he would make in speaking of his standards as an artist. The unity of Faulkner's work would seem to be implicit in these words in the concluding paragraph of his acceptance address:

> I decline to accept the end of man. . . . I believe that man will not only endure, he will prevail. He is immortal . . . because he has a soul, a spirit capable of compassion and sacrifice and endurance. The poet's, the writer's duty is to write about these things.

The important word here is "man." Compassion, sacrifice, endurance, as well as "love and honor and pity and pride" are characteristics of individuals, not of peoples. If the writer is to give them meaning he must find them first of all in his characters, not in society. Society, man, will endure only as long as individuals are capable of enduring.

But Faulkner's speech is still merely a statement of the writer's duty. These are the human values he must write about. But how, if he does not hold them true for himself? Faulkner has been accused of failing in his characterizations because he does not believe in them.[4] It would seem that this objection must be answered, since it is impossible for a man to write convincingly of something of which he is not himself convinced. What are Faulkner's own standards? What does he, the man, not the writer, think Man should do and be? Answer to this comes in an address made in the summer of 1951 to the graduating class of the Oxford, Mississippi high school—incidentally, Faulkner's second public appearance since the Stockholm speech. It is quoted here in part, as printed in *The Christian Science Monitor* under the title "An Author's Adjuration."

> What threatens us today is fear. Not the atom bomb, nor even fear of it, because if the bomb fell on Oxford tonight, all it could do would be to kill us, which is nothing, since in doing that, it will have robbed itself of its only power over us: which is fear of it, the being afraid of it. Our danger is not that. Our danger is the forces in the world today, which are trying to use man's fear to rob him of his individuality, his soul, trying to reduce him to an unthinking mass by fear and bribery—giving him free food which he has not earned, easy and valueless money which he has not worked for;—the economies of ideologies or political systems. Communist or Socialist or Democratic, whatever they wish to call themselves, the tyrants and the politicians, American or European or Asiatic, whatever they call themselves, who would reduce man to one obedient mass for their own aggrandisement and power, or because they themselves are baffled and afraid, afraid of, or incapable of believing in man's capacity for courage and endurance and sacrifice.

That is what we must resist, if we are to change the world for man's peace and security. It is not man in the mass who can and will save Man~~,~~ it is Man himself, created in the image of God so that he shall have the power and the will to choose right from wrong and so be able to save himself because he is worth saving;—Man the individual, men and women, who will always refuse to be tricked or frightened or bribed into surrendering, not just the right but the duty too, to choose between justice and injustice, courage and cowardice, sacrifice and greed, pity and self;—who will believe always not only in the right of man to be free of injustice and rapacity and deception, but the duty of man to see that justice and truth and pity and compassion are done.

So, never be afraid. Never be afraid to raise your voice for honesty and truth and compassion against injustice and lying and greed. If you, not just you in this room tonight, but in all the thousands of other rooms like this one about the world today and tomorrow and next week, will do this, not as a class or classes, but as individuals, men and women, you will change the earth. In one generation all the Napoleons and Hitlers and Caesars and Mussolinis and Stalins, and all the other tyrants who want power and aggrandisement, and the simple politicians and time-servers who themselves are merely baffled or ignorant or afraid, who have used or are using, or hope to use, man's fear and greed for man's enslavement will have vanished from the face of it.[5]

So, then, the writer is to write about the things which Faulkner believes most important to man himself. It is only as man is aware of his duty and his responsibility to "choose between justice and injustice, courage and cowardice, sacrifice and greed, pity and self" that the world may be changed for man's peace and security and for his salvation. And a man can be aware of that duty and responsibility only as he has "a soul, a spirit capable of compassion and sacrifice and endurance." The representation of that awareness or of the lack of it must be the writer's theme. It is the only significant one he can have or that Faulkner believes he should have. It must necessarily be the story he himself is trying to tell.

Since Faulkner has told us what he is trying to do, it becomes important to find out to what extent he has succeeded. He has now produced a large enough body of work, both novels and short stories, to make it possible to form some sort of judgment of the assertion he is making and to evaluate it in terms of his narrative. To what extent readers agree with that assertion is of no consequence, but it is of the greatest consequence that they should know what Faulkner's view is and should recognize it in his work.

We must begin with certain points clearly understood and seen as subjects to be developed within this essay. First, Faulkner is important both for what he has to say and for the way he says it. Therefore his work should be the concern not only of critics and students but of the large group of intelligent readers who understand and appreciate good novels. It is these readers, however, who have been discouraged by reviews often so involved in recondite questions of style that they are almost incomprehensible, or by the sections devoted to Faulkner in studies of modern American literature. Since most of the latter were written before the appearance of some of Faulkner's major work, the authors have not had enough material to consider and have made fatally discouraging generalizations. But, according to George Snell, one of Faulkner's chief deterrents has been the bookseller, who has accused Faulkner of morbidity, moral unreliability, and unintelligibility. As Snell heatedly says,

The unacknowledged censor of our literature is the ignorant bookstore clerk; and he is also far more powerful in shaping popular literary opinion than any Samuel Johnson.[6]

Of course Faulkner has his devoted readers, but they are few in number. He is generally classified as that elite of elites, a "critic's novelist." For much of the reading public that is the novelist's sentence of death.

The second consideration which must be kept in mind is that Faulkner has made mistakes. He is a prolific writer, and, like any author whose output is large, he is not always successful. He has written some bad novels — witness *Sanctuary* and *Mosquitoes* — and some unfortunate short stories. If, however, it is found that on the whole he has accomplished what he set out to do, some mistakes may be forgiven him.

It is only fair to the critics and to the hesitant public to remember another fact. Until Faulkner received the Nobel prize he had made no statement of what he was trying to do, with the exception of a short introduction to the Modern Library edition of *Sanctuary*, one of his more lurid productions. There he said only that he had written the book for money, that he expected it to shock people, but that he hoped they would buy it.[7] They did buy, and it did shock. Afterward Faulkner remained silent. Readers thoroughly frightened by their *Sanctuary* experience had little inclination to find out that subsequent novels were not just more of the same.

Since 1926, then, when *Soldiers' Pay* appeared, and Faulkner became a critical gold mine, there has been little to guide judgment of him. This is apparent in the study of criticism of his work. Articles have appeared steadily, until they compose a sizeable bibliography. Considered as a whole they reflect a strange kind of anger, as if the gentlemen were suffering a mixture of hurt feelings and extreme irritation. The brethren seem to feel that there is *something* important there, but they cannot agree upon what it is. They admit with reservations that Faulkner's technique is formidable and remarkable but what he is doing with it is the question.

Critics have been laboring, however, under two severe handicaps: lack of knowledge of Faulkner's intention and lack of fictional performance by Faulkner when they began to work. Very few articles consider more than one or two books, or, as in *The Portable Faulkner*, excerpts from several. Reviews were inspired by the appearance of each new novel, but it was only after many had been published that the relationships from book to book were perceived.

Now Faulkner's work may be considered less haphazardly. He has published enough to give readers a fairly clear idea of his method and his plan and he has himself made perfectly plain what he wants his work to accomplish. There are new cards on the table, more pieces to fit into the puzzle. It is the purpose of this paper to play the game a little further to try to reach more comprehensive conclusions about Faulkner's achievement in the body of his fiction as a unified work. It is also the purpose of this paper to attempt to solve some of the problems which confront a reader new to Faulkner's writing, and to see beyond the difficulties some of his technical devices may present to the ways in which those devices serve to make Faulkner's development of his theme more interesting and meaningful. This explanation is necessary if his achievement artistically as well as ethically is to be understood.

In approaching the study of Faulkner's fiction it seems important to answer the following questions: What are the generally accepted standards for the ingredients of fiction? What have critics had to say about Faulkner's methods of using and developing each of them? What are Faulkner's actual methods? And finally how has his technique furthered or failed to further his artistic intention? It seems certain that no serious writer wishes deliberately to confuse his readers. Unhappily, because of some admittedly unusual qualities in Faulkner's work, obscurity is often the result he has achieved. It may be argued that if a writer is so difficult to understand either in idea or method he cannot be worth reading, and that possibility ought to be carefully considered. The other side, however, deserves equal consideration: the possibility that after examination it may develop that Faulkner is not as obscure and involved as he has been made to sound and that his individual methods of handling characterization, situation, chronology, and dialogue may have the virtue of increasing the impact of his writing.

THE first question to be answered concerns the purpose of the novel as a literary type. What is it supposed to do for the reader? If we consider the work of great novelists we see in it what DeVoto calls the assertion of "some magnificent simplicity: doom precipitated or doom averted, desire fulfilled or unfulfilled, cruelty or tenderness triumphant, the world conquering or the world conquered, life stable or life flowing away."[8] In other words, the work of the novel is to show experience. That experience, Trilling says, should help a reader to "penetrate snobbery and reach the truth behind false appearances,"[9] for in his definition the work of the novel is as an "agent of moral imagination."[10] He considers that the value of a novel of moral imagination is that it "involves the reader in his own moral life," "invites him to examine his own motives," shows him that "reality is not as he sees it," points out the "extent of human variety" and the value of such variety, and cultivates in a reader "understanding and forgiveness."[11] This is also the position held by Beach, who says that the "appeal of fiction must be simultaneously to the heart, imagination, and mind."[12]

It is interesting that all these writers stress the moral element in the novel. Although, as Miss Drew says, "uncertainty has revolutionized the moral outlook" to the point where "right and wrong are less clear,"[13] it is nevertheless true that many readers expect in a novel evidences of moral standards of some kind on the author's part. They wish him to believe in *something*, not to "view human behavior with anesthetized tolerance and glacial pessimism" as Hartwick has accused Faulkner of doing.[14] Most readers, whether they would admit it or not, have their own moral standards, and while they may not necessarily expect a novelist to agree with them, they may wish to be given an opportunity to respect an opposite view. They contribute their own views as they read, and wish to believe that the writer is doing the same.

When Maxwell Geismar said, "Faulkner has the talent for the malicious in its purest form among contemporary writers,"[15] he was using an unequivocal word to describe the difficulty which many critics have felt in Faulkner's writing. Malice is a weak reed indeed for any author to lean upon, and if malice has been at the back of what Faulkner has been doing it is no wonder that critics and readers have felt antagonism toward his work. Faulkner's own statement, however, should alter the picture radically. It is not possible to deal with truths of the human heart, as he says he must, in a spirit of malice. And it ought to be possible for a reader to see in considering the themes of his fiction that Faulkner is appealing to heart and imagination and mind and through them to moral convictions, and that he is doing it by every device at his command.

It is difficult to see, for example, how the heart can resist such a story as "The Bear"—the tenderly told, symbolic account of the growing up of a boy to manhood and to the responsibilities of the adult world. The imagination is stimulated by Faulkner's accounts of life in the days of the Chickasaws—"Red Leaves," "A Justice," "A Courtship," and "Lo!" And the mind finds something to work on in the collection of detective stories in *Knight's Gambit*. The appeal here as well as in nearly all Faulkner's work comes not only from the writing but from the sense of inner conviction which he imparts to his readers, from his own belief in the value of the truths of the human heart.

FAULKNER'S METHODS

Character Presentation

Since Faulkner has chosen fiction as his medium, another of the criteria against which his success or failure must be measured is his understanding and use of fictional forms. The term "novel" carries a definite meaning, and although the novelist is freer than other writers to innovate, he must still conform to certain conventions if he wishes to be understood.

A novel, generally considered, is a work of fiction with its emphasis upon contemporary character and the realization of that character through situation, mood, and action. Emphasis may be upon any of the three, but a reader is seldom confused as to which type of novel he is reading—that is until he comes to a writer like Faulkner. Much of the critical dilemma Faulkner has caused appeared at this point. Many critics have been so struck by the frequent horror or depravity of his situations, the gloom and pessimism of his mood, the seeming inexplicability of his characters' actions, or the difficulty of his style that they have had little to say about the characters as they have been revealed. They have seen Faulkner's people as "dominated by obsession,"[16] "acting under compulsion toward predestined ends,"[17] "brooders with prodigious memories,"[18] "mechanically damned,"[19] "molds for fantastic qualities,"[20] qualities acting out a myth,"[21] "unable to grow up because they have no world to grow up into,"[22] "invariably deviations from the norm,"[23] "presented at an unwavering pitch of absolute desperation and damnation."[24] There is nothing here of "courage and sacrifice and pity."

Yet Faulkner says these are the only important things, these are the things he is writing about. Therefore he must be using situation, mood, and action as the background against which his characters display the qualities he believes in. Do his stories reveal these qualities?

We ought to grant the probability that Faulkner, like any other serious artist, is doing in his way what he says he must. But discovering this view of experience in Faulkner does take careful thinking and an approach that is not needed in the study of the ordinary novel. As any reader opens a new book he is expecting to meet new people—not impossible or unbelievable, but new to him at least for implications or heightened insight. These characters will be found in a clearly defined situation; and as it develops they will develop too. Some readers, especially those raised in the tradition of such writers as Hardy and Conrad, will also anticipate that author comment and answers on abstractions will show them what their own feelings toward these new individuals should be. Many others do not feel this need. They prefer the author who, as Elizabeth Drew says, believes in "the right of every soul to find its own salvation"[25] and offers his readers no judgment of values and morality. If, however, a reader does wish to understand the characters as the author sees them, he considers it the author's obligation to have conveyed these meanings clearly by the end of the book.

It is of the utmost importance that the beginning reader be aware of Faulkner's method of character presentation. Faulkner requires a different attitude entirely. His readers must get into the mood they feel when they move to a new town. We have all had that experience. We know we do not meet and know everyone all at once, even if someone has a party for us. At the moment of our arrival we are at an intermediate moment in the life of the town itself. Certain things have already happened about which we know nothing. Some things—love affairs, family feuds, business quarrels—are in progress. Some things we see happen are due to long-gone almost forgotten causes. Some people we come to know very well almost at once. Others we only just meet. We may get to know them later. Sometimes we may not ever find out much. We hear conversations that do not mean anything to us, but we find out later those few sentences have meant a great deal to someone else. We never realize what anyone is like, or capable of, until something we consider a crisis occurs. Sometimes crises occur but we do not recognize them. Perhaps we leave that town and do not return for years. When we do, we realize the meaning of much we had missed before. We reverse many of our decisions of the earlier period and we make many new ones.

Any novel reader knows that he is being told a "permissive lie" as DeVoto calls it.[26] The difference between Faulkner's novels and those of other writers is that a reader is asked for more "willing suspension of disbelief" than that to which he is accustomed. Faulkner says, in effect, "This story may seem to you to be beginning in the middle. The answers to many things you do not understand are in another book. Some of the characters may not seem important, but they really are. Just at this particular moment in time, and in this situation they are not taking a prominent part, so that you may not feel you know them very well. They are important, however, because they are individuals, and their complete stories will be told at the proper time. After you have lived here awhile you will come to know them."

This is a promise that Faulkner keeps. When the reader has followed him long enough he finds that he has learned much about a large group of people. Most important of what he has learned is that some of these characters understand courage and pride and pity and some do not. He has also learned why they are the sort of people they are, because they have been so fully presented that he cannot fail to comprehend them.

It is apparent, therefore, that in order to do justice to Faulkner's characterization a reader may not isolate one book from any other, nor leave the short stories alone while he considers the novels. Faulkner's work must be thought of as a block rather than as a series of parts. It may be started anywhere, because it has no beginning; it may end anywhere because it has no ending; but it must be looked at completely. It is not the story of a day or a year or a lifetime. It is life and time, because it is primarily the story of people. And it is precisely because Faulkner's concern is with individuals that it is dangerous to attempt generalizations beyond what he has himself said about his ideas of social or moral truth or about his artistic purpose—that he is interested in and writing about "man"—the individual.

Use of Point of View

The significance of Faulkner's method of characterization becomes more apparent when we consider another aspect of his presentation. One of the problems confronting the novelist is to decide the point of view from which he will tell his story. The author may choose to be omniscient, to be equally aware of both the thoughts and the actions of every character in the story, to have in his view the whole panorama. He may choose to observe and evaluate from within the mind of one character, either one of major importance, whose actions and reactions influence the development of the plot, or one of minor significance, who merely notes the surface of events without himself having any power to direct their course. Another possibility is to have the story actually told by one of the characters. In all but the first method a reader may easily identify himself with the author's chosen character and may easily share his point of view. Such identification is also possible in the story told by the omniscient author as long as the character in question holds the center of the stage. When the lead shifts to another character, however, a reader must shift his attention too.

There are advantages and disadvantages to each method. In the story told by the omniscient author the reader stands above and looks down. "Every side is equally wrought and fashioned," Percy Lubbock says.[27] When the center of vision is in one of the characters "one side is in the rough"[28]—the side that character cannot see. Sometimes it is useful to have the author as narrator, especially when a descriptive picture is needed,[29] but as Lubbock sees the problem, the stronger method is to place the center of gravity in the life of the character rather than to make the story "merely a reflection of life beyond and outside him."[30]

9

In present day writing the choice is generally for the author to sub-merge himself in one of the characters to such a degree that the reader is almost completely unaware that the author is speaking. Another convention to which modern readers have become accustomed is the author's staying in that one character throughout the book; and a third is that the author will select for himself a character whose reactions are within the range of "normal" experience—normal in that for most read-ers these reactions are recognizable, frequently met, and unsensational. Here again Faulkner asks more of most readers than they are prepared to give unless they are warned.

At first glance it seems that Faulkner is following the modern custom and keeping himself out of the picture. We appear to be reading a story told from the point of view of one of the characters. Then we realize that the character is thinking, sometimes speaking, but more often think-ing, in terms which seem inconsistent with his age or race or with the situation in which he finds himself. We are unaccustomed to sixteen-year-olds who think this way:

because it was not empty at all now, deserted and empty of movement certainly running as vacant of life from street lamp to street lamp as a dead street through an abandoned city but not really abandoned not really withdrawn but only making way for them who could do it better, only making way for them who could do it right, not to interfere or get in the way or even offer suggestions or even permit (with thanks) advice to them who would do it right and in their own homely way since it was their own grief and their own shame and their own expiation.[31]

Nor do we readily expect as mature a philosophy as this from a ten-year-old:

He stopped for the first time since he had arisen from the log when he could see the compass face at last, and looked about, mopping his sweating face on his sleeve. He had already relinquished, of his will, because of his need, in humility and peace and without regret, yet apparently that had not been enough, the leaving of the gun was not enough. He stood for a moment—a child alien and lost in the green and soaring gloom of the markless wilderness. Then he relinquished completely to it. It was the watch and the compass. He was still tainted. He removed the linked chain of the one and the looped thong of the other from his overalls and hung them on a bush and leaned the stick beside them and entered.[32]

And young men and their fathers do not often hold quite such symbolic discussion as this on the subject of light to read by:

"You will probably have to go inside to read it," Mr. Compson said.
"Maybe I can read it here all right," Quentin said.
"Perhaps you are right," Mr. Compson said. "Maybe even the light of day, let alone this—" he indicated the single globe stained and bug-fouled from the long summer and which even when clean gave off but little light—"would be too much for it, for them. Yes, for them: of that day and time, of a dead time; people too as we are, and victims too as we are, but victims of a different circumstance, simpler and therefore, integer for integer, larger, more heroic and the figures therefore more heroic too, not dwarfed and involved but distinct, uncomplex who had the gift of loving once or dying once instead of being diffused and scattered creatures drawn blindly limb from limb from a grab bag and assembled, author and victim too of

a thousand homicides and a thousand copulations and divorcements. Perhaps you are right. Perhaps any more light than this would be too much for it."[33]

The result of this depth which seems beyond the character's capacities and beyond the significance of the situation may be a sense of resentment, if not of resistance; a feeling that Faulkner is taking an unfair advantage of his readers, that instead of creating his characters and letting them exist in their own right he is intruding to give his own instead of the characters' logical answers to the problems his stories raise.

In other instances Faulkner may present his narrative from successive points of view, shifting from character to character throughout the book. Much of *Light in August* is told from the view of Byron Bunch; some of the action is seen by Joe Christmas himself; Hightower has a large share. The same thing is true of *Absalom, Absalom!*, of *The Hamlet*, and of *As I Lay Dying*. The latter book has been criticized by Snell because "the reader is not well prepared and is unable to suspend disbelief as in a continuous narrative."[34] On the other hand it is praised by Linn and Taylor in *A Foreword to Fiction* as an illustration of the "breaking up of the surface by shifting points of view while keeping the center of the simple story."[35]

Key to Faulkner's technique in *As I Lay Dying* would seem upon examination to be that it is indeed a "simple story." Told in the customary way from the point of view of only one of the characters it would lose a great deal of the force it acquires as the changing situations are seen from the point of view of each of the characters involved. It is true that a reader does have to dodge back and forth from one character to another, but if we analyze the story it may be seen how effective this demand is.

Faulkner has told us that he wishes to write about the truths of the human heart. In *As I Lay Dying* he selects as his characters the members of the Bundren family and a group of their neighbors. These people are "poor whites." They live a scrawny life on their poor farms in a far corner of the county. Their wants are few, because they have little idea of all the things they might possibly want. Looked at objectively they are unattractive, even repulsive; a sympathetic reader would probably feel a desire to teach them new agricultural methods and personal cleanliness. He would never feel like identifying himself with them.

That, however, is just what Faulkner asks his readers to do. A reader enters the story just as Mrs. Bundren is at the point of death. Outside, under the window, her son Cash is making her coffin, and the noise of hammer and saw fills the hot room. Cash is working desperately to make the best coffin he can with the materials he has. There is no other way to get a coffin, or if there is Cash does not know it. In various states of unhappiness the other members of the family are waiting for Addie to die. Her husband is chiefly resentful, in the realization that he is being put to great inconvenience. Her youngest son, Vardaman, is curious about what she will turn into. Jewel has his heart and his mind more on his horse; Dewey Dell is more concerned over her undoubted pregnancy; and Darl's interest is in the quality of his own sorrow. None of them is appealing as we meet them.

Then Addie dies. The coffin is finished, the funeral is over. And now the family sets out to solve the most demanding problem it has ever confronted. Before her death the Bundrens had promised Addie that she would be buried in the graveyard in Jefferson, the town she had left as a bride. Stated that way, it seems simple. Just ship the body there, and have it buried. Or, if that seems too difficult, forget the promise. This promise, however, the keeping or not keeping of it, presents an overwhelming ethical and moral demand to the Bundrens. They are an unlikely lot, ignorant and slovenly, but unlikely as they seem, they have within them a respect for the human values Faulkner admires. They are in a situation which seems ridiculous and bizarre. For them it is fraught with meaning which the nicer decisions of life could never have. Their grief for Addie herself is not great enough to move them, since for their kind grief is a luxury. Keeping themselves alive takes all their time. Their morals are subject to considerations of expediency. But of this one thing they are sure: Addie must be buried as she had wished and as they have promised.

If a reader manages to understand this and has grasped the deep importance of the problem, the carrying out of the promise becomes his struggle as well as the Bundrens'. The dreadful difficulties of the journey, the family's persistence in spite of all obstacles, the personal troubles and triumphs of each member as a reader may get to know him through that person's mind become that reader's difficulties, his persistence, his troubles and triumphs. Even the end makes sense. Mr. Bundren has married a new wife and finally bought store teeth.

To some readers this denouement is ridiculous after the piling up of the tragedy of Darl's madness and Dewey Dell's "trouble." But if Darl's madness is his reaction to Addie's death, if Dewey Dell is in trouble because she knew no better (and never would, probably), then Mr. Bundren's hasty wedding is just as logical. His was the chief responsibility for carrying out the promise. He has done it against great odds. He is in town, a place he almost never visits. He has time to buy his new teeth, and he has met a nice woman who can take Addie's place and assure him of the care he wants for the rest of his life. It is only practical to marry her while he has the opportunity, since there is no knowing when he will have another.

The important thing is that the promise has been kept, at no matter what cost. There may not ever be another challenge like it for the Bundrens. But Faulkner has proved what he set out to prove: that in a situation requiring a choice between "justice and injustice, courage and cowardice, sacrifice and greed, pity and self" even such people as the

Bundrens can choose for the right. A reader who has read carefully knows it, too, for he has made the choice himself. He has lived inside each member of the family on the long, slow, irritating journey through the August heat; he has watched from the creaking wagon the buzzards wheeling overhead; he has felt the frustrations that were not frustrations because they could not be allowed to matter. He has not thought of judging right or wrong or of saying, even to himself, "It would be so much easier if you would just do it this way." He has done it the Bundrens' way, because for the moment that is the only way he knows.

The chief objection to Faulkner's use of the point of view, however, has arisen upon serious ethical grounds. Frequently readers find themselves being asked to understand events and situations as well as other characters from the point of view of someone who is himself abnormal. Indeed, Millett accuses Faulkner's world of being seriously "distorted by the nature of narrator."[36] Many a reader feels he has enough to do in comprehending complicated action without being asked to look at life through the eyes of a creature like Benny in *The Sound and the Fury* or Darl in *As I Lay Dying* or the idiot Snopes in *The Hamlet*. These are the most difficult, but they are at least pitiable. Others are hard to accept in terms of any ethical ideals because they are repulsive and foreign to everyday experience: Mink Snopes, Jason Compson, Temple Drake. A mature reader may well be willing to admit such people exist and may be willing to read about them, but he may be bothered by the idea of seeing so far into their minds. They may set up in some sensitive readers a fear of the potential degradation to which humanity is liable. Indeed this horror may make so deep an impression that such characters are remembered at the expense of many others anyone would be glad to know: Ratliff, Aunt Jenny, Dilsey, Gavin Stevens, Molly Beauchamp.

Obviously Faulkner must have some purpose in all this. He must intend by these characters to prove something about the truths of the human heart of which he is writing. It is fair criticism to consider them as devices and to try to understand Faulkner's reasons for using them. It is impossible to measure his achievement as a novelist unless we use the terms he uses instead of the terms we have learned to apply to some other writers. Faulkner must be his own yardstick. The question is not "Why doesn't Faulkner do what everyone else does?" but "Why does he do what he does?"

In his introduction to the Modern Library edition of *Light in August* Richard Rovere undertakes to explain one aspect of Faulkner's work which needs to be understood here:

There are some writers who make us privy to human experience; there are others who subject us to it. Faulkner . . . belongs to the second group. Those who make us privy to human experience are, among moderns, men like Shaw, Forster, Gide, Mann, Lawrence, Orwell—the teachers and the moralists of a generation. Reading them, we observe human conduct, we speculate upon it, we extend the range of our perceptions and sympathies. We can become deeply involved with the people to whom their imagination has given life, but as we do so there is never any doubt in our minds that we remain ourselves, that we have merely been put in communication with others. We may establish rapport but seldom identity.

With a writer like Faulkner, though, when we respond to him at all, we do not so much observe experience as undergo it. We do not recognize a mood; we are overcome by it. Faulkner too is a teacher and moralist . . . but his most compelling gift is for transmitting a kind of experience that is, outside of art like his, definable only in terms of itself. It is often impossible to feel *for* Faulkner's characters, but it is almost always possible to feel *with* them. . . . With Faulkner we come about as close to the assimilation of another's sensations as it is possible to come in literature, which is to say a good deal closer, than, as a rule, it is possible to come in life.[37]

Part of the answer to perplexities about Faulkner is certainly here, but it is not the whole answer. Many readers feel the same kind of identification with the characters in novels by writers who make them "privy to experience," even when those characters are entirely outside their own way of life. This sympathy, however, has seemed justified because great novelists of the past have had what DeVoto says any great novelist must have: greatness of mind and spirit.[38] This is not to say that greatness of mind and spirit have been the peculiar possessions of past novelists only; but it is their greatness of mind and spirit which has given perpetual life to their work. Such qualities give to any author a certain command over his readers. If they respond they are willing to submit to him, to believe what he tells them, even when what he tells them is outside their own experience or is unpleasant. Even if he appears to lack conventional faith, as, according to Miss Drew, many novelists of today do, or seem to do, he has developed an important individual faith in the meaning of life through greatness of mind and spirit.[39] Therefore readers, deeply moved by and for and with his characters, have also felt the purpose of that sympathy. It has had meaning for them, in the light of the author's own concept of life.

It is exactly that greatness of mind and spirit, that positive faith and concept of life which, as we have already noted, critics have denied Faulkner. Or if they have granted him a faith it has been only a dark one. Beach thinks that the only lesson to be derived from Faulkner's work is that "human behavior is too inveterately tragic and fateful to be corrected."[40] Luccock says that Faulkner seems to express the "sense of the 'abyss' under the covering of life, the horror, the malignant element in man."[41] Geismar sees a "continuing sense of destruction, incessant breeding of evil by evil."[42] There is no catharsis, he feels, through this sense of evil. There is no pattern of guilt and expiation as with the Russians or Hemingway, no tenderness, no redemption through suffering or through anything else.[43] Snell finds in Faulkner's people only "imponderable dark recesses of spirit, shadowy depths of soul, abnormal and bizarre."[44] Kazin insists that Faulkner in the end always tells the same story: "damnation leading to mysterious abject submission, leading to perdition."[45]

If these things were true, then certainly there would seem little purpose in the wringing of the heart which those readers who respond to Faulkner do feel. Much of their suffering would have to be laid to the fact that the characters with whom they were identifying themselves were hopeless of any salvation. Therefore why should they bother to read about such people? And why should they feel *with* a character it is so difficult to feel *for?*

The answer, again, is that Faulkner, by his own assertion, has a positive faith and a positive concept of life. He is expressing it through his characters. He is trying by every means possible to show it to his readers. He believes that the only way to understand people, the only way to find out what is in them of "courage and pity and pride" is to know them inside-out, not outside-in. It makes no difference who or what they are, or how we feel toward them. We must study them, good or bad, with the same depth and thoroughness.

It appears, then, that Faulkner's readers are going to have to be prepared to approach his stories from almost any angle, and to be prepared to shift, often without warning, from one point of view to another. This technique, like all the others, is justified if by using it Faulkner furthers his purpose. There is no question raised here as to which method of presentation is best. The only thing that is important is the result to be achieved: to make the reader feel and understand with the character, and through him to gain a fuller and deeper comprehension of life. If Faulkner has that purpose in mind—and he says he has—the method he selects is his own affair. His success or failure is a matter for his readers to decide.

Setting

An additional decision to be made by the author is the background against which his story will take place. He may select a typical environment: a nameless city, an unidentified country; or he may choose a specific place which a reader may identify from his own experience: New York, Chicago, Tahiti. Faulkner has combined the two methods by the creation of a Mississippi county, as Hardy created Wessex and George Barr McCutcheon the romantic Graustark. Although he has occasionally used other settings, the best of Faulkner's stories take place in Yoknapatawpha county. Its county seat is Jefferson, and its primary interest is cotton. Malcolm Cowley has described it in his introduction to the *Portable Faulkner:*

Faulkner's mythical kingdom is a country in northern Mississippi, on the border between the sand hills covered with scrubby pine and the black earth of the river bottoms. Except for the storekeepers, mechanics, and professional men who live in Jefferson, the county seat, all the inhabitants are farmers and woodsmen. Except for a little lumber, their only product is baled cotton for the Memphis market. A few of them live in big plantation houses, the relics of another age, and more of them in substantial wooden farmhouses; but most of them are tenants, no better housed than slaves on good plantations before the Civil War. Yoknapatawpha county—"William

Faulkner, sole owner and proprietor,"—as he inscribed on one of the maps be drew —has a population of 15,611 persons (whites, 6,298, negroes, 9,313[46]) scattered over 2400 square miles.[47]

Yoknapatawpha county is imaginary, but as it furnishes the setting for book after book it attains a vivid reality, so that it is hard to believe that the traveler through Mississippi will never see Jefferson with its courthouse and jail nor the cotton fields and pine woods which he has come to know through Faulkner's pen. If this limitation of setting is an aid to reality, it also has a certain danger: that many readers will come to associate characters and situation so closely with Yoknapatawpha that they will fail to see any universal application in them and will conclude that Faulkner is a "local" writer. Local color has a place in any novel and has been used effectively by many writers, although not many have been as specific and thorough as Faulkner. Ellen Glasgow, another novelist of the South, used a more generalized setting, as did Sarah Orne Jewett in New England and Willa Cather in the middle and south West. Hardy never furnished a topographical map of Wessex or supplied his readers with census figures.

In giving his more detailed picture Faulkner has gone farther than these writers but in the same direction. He is using "place and setting as important structural elements" with an inescapable bearing on characters, because he feels what Warren calls the "significance of Nature, sociology, geography and human geography."[48] As Faulkner conceives that significance it can be more clearly demonstrated if it is made specific. The factors of Yoknapatawpha county have a conditioning force, but that same force is, of course, exerted by any environment.

Actually Yoknapatawpha county has its counterparts all over the world, wherever there are people who live by the land and live poorly, whose past is greater than their present, and who have the problem of an alien race to whom justice must be done. It is through these men and women as representatives of all men and women, and through their relationships with one another that Faulkner makes his bid to prove his artistic and ethical ideas. The meaning comes as Gavin Stevens says to his young nephew:

Some things you must always be unable to bear. Some things you must never stop refusing to bear. Injustice and outrage and dishonor and shame. No matter how young you are or how old you have got.[49]

Situations

At this point readers may very well say, "Of course. That's perfectly simple. All readers know that." And, indeed, they do. Faulkner is by no means the first writer to hold such a thesis. But a reader who expects to have it proved in the usual way must again prepare himself to be surprised by Faulkner's method. This is the point at which the shock comes. Faulkner once more is asking for a different approach, a different sort of appreciation, a different concept of what a novel should be. The road to understanding of it lies through consideration of two overworked terms: "romance" and "realism."

The development of the American novel has been steadily away from the nineteenth century emphasis upon romance—stories of larger-than-life characters involved in larger-than-life situations—toward the study of real people with real problems. There have been many influences upon this development: the French writers whose realism was accepted before their American followers could achieve success; and the various challenges offered to the writer in the changing picture of America itself. The growth of industrial cities, the increasing problems of the farmers, rising class barriers, all these could not be ignored. The result has been that American writers have dealt increasingly with what they have seen around them, but at the same time they have not liked what they have seen. As Kazin puts it:

The greatest single fact about modern writing is the writer's absorption in every detail of the American world together with a deep and subtle alienation from it.[50]

As Miss Drew, an English writer, finds that in the relationship between the American novel and American civilization the writers of social criticism are in revolt against their material.[51]

Such American novels of rejection and of social complaint have, however, been popular and make up the main development since the nineties. Readers have been interested in the studies of society and of social problems which contemporary writers have given them. They have missed the point made by Trilling that what they are reading is not literature but a copying of reality.[52] Trilling believes further that the American reader has become so accustomed to this type of novel that he suspects evidences of style and thought, of plot complication, of modulations in tone, or of the personal idiosyncrasy of the author.[53] He wants photographic realism and propaganda, and nothing more.

But Faulkner persists in giving this type of realism and something more. He is indeed a realist. He is fully aware of what is going on around him, and he is often deeply alienated by what he sees. In many phases of his work, however, he is what Dr. Walter Myers calls an "extra-realist." Extra-realism is defined by Myers as an "acute consciousness of the actual with a sense of the mystic"[54] which often "leads to grotesquerie."[55] It is the logical development of the inclusion as normal of more and more that used to be considered incongruous in ideas or behavior. This has come about as the field of the normal has been expanded through science and especially through the study of psychology. Now, as Myers says, "the tendency is for realism to adopt the exceptional and extraordinary and leave romance only the impossible."[56]

That idea may not be difficult to accept in theory, but not very many novel readers have it in mind when they begin a new book. They are prepared for new people, as has been said, and they may be willing to meet them in the new way Faulkner requires, but at least the things that happen to them should be the sort of things that happen to anyone. Again, however, Faulkner presents a special problem, asks a further suspension of disbelief. This time he says, in effect: "You may find it hard to believe that these things could happen in real life. Perhaps they cannot—or at least they will not—to you. But something will present the same sort of challenge to you. It will be different in form, perhaps, but not in reality and intensity."

Thus reading Faulkner becomes a difficult task. A reader must keep his mental balance as he follows his new acquaintances in and out of situations that are sometimes so startling on the surface that he can concentrate on nothing else. The boy in *Intruder in the Dust* seems like a normal teen-ager; but that is easy to forget when a reader finds him exhuming corpses at midnight to save a Negro from a lynching. It seems like distorted boy-scouting. Temple Drake is a nasty girl who is raped. That should serve her right, but she has no business enjoying it. The convict in "Old Man" behaves well in a trying adventure. What is the point of his choosing to return to the jail when he could have escaped? After all the anguish of *The Wild Palms* why not let the young doctor commit suicide? Why must he "take grief"? Why devote a whole book to the adventures of a family of seeming zanies hauling a putrefying corpse all over Mississippi in the middle of August? Why lavish pages of description on the love affair of an idiot and a cow?

Of course a reader is startled. Often he is horrified. His recollection of the book as a whole is spoiled by the memory of those obtrusive incidents which seem only grotesque, overdone, needlessly shocking. This is where, in fairness to the author, readers must take another and a longer look. What does Faulkner mean? Is he being merely sensational, is he the victim of his own obsessions, is he laughing malignly at life, or is he saying something about the values he feels are true?

Again it is well to forget the critics and look at the books themselves. We know they are about a specified group of people and their relationships with one another. What do they show us further? Perhaps as we study the individual problem each book presents and tries to solve we may see Faulkner's pattern of meaning emerging from the incongruous incidents. Here we must decide whether to follow the chronology of Yoknapatawpha county and its people or the development and biography of Faulkner as a writer. In the latter analysis we discover the history of a talent, in the former the history of an idea. The study is better criticism and is more important if we try to determine the idea as it can be developed from the internal evidence of the stories themselves. As we follow the narrative we may find out how the "refusing or not refusing to bear injustice and dishonor and outrage and shame" have persisted and been made manifest from the beginning of the county's history to the present in the lives of its people and the conduct they have chosen. And we may also discover why the choice between good and evil has been presented in situations many readers find unusual.

The history of the county goes back to the days when the land that is now Yoknapatawpha belonged to a tribe of Chickasaws. Incoming settlers bought or robbed them of their heritage until the day of the great Indian resettlement to the West, when the Chickasaws left behind them only the halfbreed descendants of their illegitimate unions with the negro slaves of the new plantation owners. This was the first crime of the white man—the buying and selling of something to which he had no right. This is the crime which Ike McCaslin seeks to expiate when he refuses to accept his heritage of land.

> I can't repudiate it. It was never mine to repudiate. It was never Father's and Uncle Buddy's to bequeathe me to repudiate, because it was never Grandfather's to bequeathe them to bequeathe me to repudiate, because it was never old Ikkemotubbe's to sell to Grandfather for bequeathement and repudiation. Because it was never Ikkemotubbe's father's father's to bequeathe Ikkemotubbe to sell to Grandfather or any man because on the instant when Ikkemotubbe discovered, realized that he could sell it for money, on that instant it ceased ever to have been his forever, father to father to father, and the man who bought it bought nothing. . . .
>
> Bought nothing. Because He told in the Book how He created the earth, made it and looked at it and said it was all right, and then He made man. He made the earth first and peopled it with dumb creatures, and then He created man to be His overseer on the earth and to hold suzerainty over the earth and the animals on it in His name, not to hold for himself and his descendants inviolable title forever, generation after generation, to the oblongs and squares of the earth, but to hold the earth mutual and intact in the communal anonymity of brotherhood, and all the fee He asked was pity and humility and sufferance and endurance and the sweat of his face for bread.[57]

But this expiation came much later. In those early days, as Faulkner has described them in a number of related short stories, the people of Jefferson and the county were interested not in ethical values but in making homes and a living.

Thus came the greater crime of slavery. The South had "erected its economic edifice not on the rock of stern morality but on the shifting sand of opportunism and moral brigandage."[58] Because the old order did not satisfy human needs, cursed as it was by slavery, it "sowed the seeds of its own ruin."[59] It is the road back from that ruin, the expiation of that crime that is still the problem of the South as Faulkner sees it. And it is the expiation as it is practiced, as in *Intruder in the Dust*, or not practiced, as in *Light in August*, which Faulkner frequently uses to illustrate his theme.

It would seem a critical fallacy, however, to assume that because Faulkner concentrates his attention upon the peculiar difficulties of the South he is writing a "human tragedy of the South, Mississippi, and Jefferson,"[60] or a "parable or legend of all the deep South."[61] What he is attempting is much more universal in application. The crime of man against man, the struggle of justice against injustice, of courage against cowardice, of sacrifice against greed, of pity against self goes on everywhere and always. Slavery is just an example, and it is the example Faulkner has chosen to use; but he is fully aware that he could have used others. It is avoiding the issue he raises if a reader sees only the South in his books, and thinks his people are only Southerners with consequently only Southern problems to solve.

The Civil War was the beginning of the long road to work out the atonement Faulkner sees as a universal problem.

'It won't be much longer now and then there won't be anything left: we wont even have anything to do left, not even the privilege of walking slowly backward for a reason, for the sake of honor and what's left of pride. Not God; evidently we have done without Him for four years, only He just didn't think to notify us; and not only not shoes and clothing but not even any need for them, and not only no land nor any way to make food, but no need for the food since we have learned to live without that too; and so if you dont have God and you dont need food and clothes and shelter, there isn't anything for honor and pride to climb on and hold to and flourish. And if you haven't got honor and pride, then nothing matters. Only there is something in you that doesn't care about honor and pride yet that lives, that even walks backward for a whole year just to live; that probably when this is over and there is not even defeat left will still decline to sit in the sun and die, but will be out in the woods, moving and seeking where just will and endurance could not move it, grubbing for roots and such.'[62]

So the people of Yoknapatawpha county, after sharing in almost four years of false victory for the forces of wrong, "walked backward slowly" in a final year of inevitable and deserved defeat, surrendered, and came home to see what was left. It was an uneasy homecoming. There were the slaves, now slaves no longer, but more of a problem because suddenly they had no one to look after them. Their former owners, themselves impoverished, were forced to do business with poor whites whom they had always disregarded. Often, too, these plantation-trained aristocrats were compelled to the losing side in their efforts at reconstruction because they had never before had to struggle to stay alive and did not understand the technique the poor white had learned through long experience. There were Northerners, too, whose money talked but who were otherwise incomprehensible. There were devastated homes and ruined acres. There were old truths to forget and new ones to learn. And there were only themselves to do it all. It took generations.

Some succeeded and some failed. The boy who rescued Lucas Beauchamp learned his lesson well. The men who killed Joe Christmas did not. The Compsons accepted defeat; the Sartorises could have won through if there had not been another war. Thomas Sutpen lost his dream and his life because he persisted in trying to save both. The Snopeses proved the truth of the turning worm.

It was the same with the rest of the county. Everyone in some measure or other faced the necessity of realizing that the old ways were gone and could never return. Some lived on in the dream of White supremacy, some emerged. Some worked for the future, some haunted the past. Faulkner has told their stories—plantation owners, poor whites, freed negroes, their children and grandchildren. And if the incidents and situations Faulkner has used seem strange and often confusing, his methods serve paradoxically to make his purpose clearer. The problem, the question of right and wrong, is frequently so evident that its statement could pass unnoticed unless it were thus dramatically presented.

It seems possible to argue, then, that because Faulkner's thesis is deceptively simple he has chosen to go beyond simplicity in illustrating it. His method is unquestionably difficult for anyone comfortably familiar with realistic presentation of life, but it can hardly be considered an unfair barrier to understanding his meaning. Actually no situation in any story of Faulkner's should be surprising to a reader of the daily paper. On the other hand readers may say that the mood in which one reads the newspaper is not the mood one should bring to a novel; and this is of course true. Here it might be well to note Cowley's suggestion that on second reading of Faulkner the "horrors are still there, but we pay more attention to the situations causing them and resulting from them."[63] In other words, we may discover that Faulkner is not using horrors as horrors—for their shock value—but as the causes or results of more significant matters—as steps in the choice between justice and injustice, courage and cowardice, sacrifice and greed, pity and self.

FAULKNER'S VIEW OF LIFE

Horror

The emphasis which readers have placed upon Faulkner's horror, morbidity, disillusionment, and pessimism is so great that it is necessary now to see just exactly to what extent they color his writing. Faulkner himself has said that he believes that part of the mature view of human experience the novelist must show lies in the realization and appreciation of important human values: courage and honor and hope and pride and compassion and pity and sacrifice. We have seen that he has tried to present them through a narrative unity of characters, setting, and idea. We have said that as a serious author he must be appealing to heart, imagination, and mind. But is Faulkner's presentation one-sided? Does he know nothing but intensity and violence? Or have his novels qualities of spirit? Does he write for the quiet moments of the heart, or is he only intent upon suffering? May we ever smile or laugh, or must we be forever plunged in gloom? May we ever feel sadness or must it always be anguish and horror? May we ever find

21

ourselves in peaceful backwaters or are we always to be tossed about on the open and unfriendly seas?

These are legitimate questions and any reader has the right to ask them. There are many great novels, novels with little stress and no horrors, which have stood the test of time and have succeeded in bringing to their readers the same truths Faulkner says he is seeking. He has attempted innovations in form and method which are not worth accepting unless they can be justified artistically and ethically. If all they achieve is resentment and confusion and weariness their value is hard to defend. If, having tried to comprehend Faulkner, a mature and sophisticated reader still feels unrewarded, the author has failed on ethical as well as on esthetic grounds.

Understanding of Faulkner's ethical achievement involves consideration of his view of life as it is disclosed through his characters and their stories. Reading a novel is a two-way affair in which a reader makes the contribution of his own view and personality.[64] He in turn, according to DeVoto, is building an illusion under the guidance of the novelist.[65] For that reason it is up to the novelist to persuade a reader to believe what he says. This, however, would seem difficult if not impossible for a novelist whose work cannot supply a strong and satisfactory answer to the question Miss Drew says is the most important one about a novel: the type of the author's mind and the depth and breadth of his experience.[66]

As an approach to the ethics of Faulkner's work, let us recall that both novelist and critic in the past have written about the duty of the novelist as artist, and it would seem wise to consider here some of the things they have said in connection with what Faulkner has done. It is these standards which readers have learned to trust.

Writing at a time when there were few novels to consider and when the form, separate from the "romance," had not existed long enough to have a past, Samuel Johnson had this to say to aspiring writers:

It ought to be the first endeavour of a writer to distinguish nature from custom, or that which is established because it is right from that which is right only because it is established: that he may neither violate essential principles by a desire of novelty nor debar himself from the attainment of beauties within his view by a needless fear of breaking rules which no literary dictator has authority to enact.[67]

It would no doubt seem to Johnson that Faulkner was taking drastic liberties in his "endeavour to distinguish nature from custom," but it may fairly be argued that he is doing no more than he has a right to do. One of Faulkner's chief concerns is to show "that which is established because it is right" as distinguished from that "which is right only because it is established." That is why the convict returns to jail at the end of *Old Man*. It is established because it is right that a man should not be forced to live where he must be unhappy. The convict is happiest at the prison farm, plowing the plot of ground that is his particular charge. Because it is established, it does not follow that it is right that a man who has a chance to escape from prison must do so, whether or not he wishes. One is nature, the other is custom. In a similar way in *The Wild Palms,* it is right that a man should suffer for harm he has done. That is therefore established. It does not follow, indeed it cannot follow, that if he has an opportunity to escape from life he must take it, although custom would condone such an act. It is established because it is right that a man may dig for gold if he wants to, as Lucas Beauchamp does in "The Fire on the Hearth." It is not right because it is established that his wife must accept what she regards as the ruin of her home because there might be money in it. When Faulkner's characters seem to be acting illogically it is well to try to find the distinction the author is making between nature and custom. Many times in life what is right because it is established and what is established because it is right are the same. In such experiences the choice between justice and injustice, courage and cowardice, sacrifice and greed, pity and self is an obvious one. At other times, however, the choice made on pragmatic grounds would be fundamentally wrong. It is then that "nature," standards of right and wrong, and not merely custom must prevail, unless, of course, we consider "slice of life" novels in which the aim is only "representation."

Henry James, to whom Faulkner has been likened, also has advice for the novelist:

Enjoy (the novelist's freedom) as it deserves; take possession of it, explore it to its utmost extent, publish it, rejoice in it. All life belongs to you, and do not listen either to those who would shut you up into corners of it and tell you that it is only here and there that art inhabits, or to those who would persuade you that this heavenly messenger wings her way outside of life together, breathing a superfine air, and turning away her head from the truth of things. There is no impression of life, no manner of seeing it and feeling it, to which the plan of the novelist may not offer a place.[68]

Such a statement would seem to justify Faulkner's use of material which has seemed in dubious taste to critics. He has a right to find the habitation of art in a raging flood or in a midnight graveyard, in a tumbledown shanty or the town jail, in a forest or a cotton field, since all of them are the "truth of things" and all of them may give impressions. He has the further right to see them and feel them as he wishes.

But the problem goes beyond the mere selection of the material. There is the effect of the novel to consider, and to that point Miss Drew says:

One of the most important questions in a serious novelist's work is whether his vision adds to a harmonized balanced view of human existence, or whether it really narrows it by emphasizing only some one aspect of life, of which he has become suddenly and extravagantly conscious.[69]

This, of course, is the heart of the criticism of Faulkner—that he has narrowed his view of life to include only the evil of it of which he is "suddenly and extravagantly conscious." In a sense he is deeply conscious of evil, but in a more positive way than the critics imply. His primary concern, after all, is to show that a man must choose between right and wrong, for one set of human values and against another. The choosing must inevitably involve conflict, which, indeed, is one of the necessary ingredients of any story./But if we can differentiate among the various qualities which together make up "good," then "evil" may be departmentalized. To tell a story of courage the writer must also make clear the possibility of abject fear. If he writes of honor, he must also write of dishonor. Hope suggests possible despair; pride, vanity; compassion, inhumanity; pity, mercilessness; and sacrifice, base selfpreservation. Failing to show or to make implicit these opposites the writer also fails to impart to his readers the intensity of experience they are seeking.

It has evidently seemed to critics that Faulkner has overdone his presentation of the obverse. It is true that in many instances in his work the form which the opposition to the forces of good has taken seems to be beyond normal experience. There are comparatively few people, for example, who have ever had to decide for or against taking part in or condoning a lynching. A woman is seldom faced with the necessity of returning to a home in which she knows her husband is waiting to kill her. Young girls are rarely confronted with the question of whether or not to go through with a marriage to a man hopelessly maimed in body and mind. But hatred and fear and repugnance are not emotions foreign to anyone's experience. We are not fond of feeling them, but they are not beyond our understanding. And they are certainly part of any harmonized view of human existence. Faulkner deals with them, as any artist must, and if he makes them seem intense, then he has succeeded in making his readers feel.

If Faulkner makes his readers deeply aware of evil, however, it is important to discover to what extent he makes real the forces of good. Where in *Light in August* or *Soldier's Pay* is the sense of love or mercy, where in "That Evening Sun" do we find courage to oppose fear? The answer in *Light in August* is in the character of Hightower, the unfrocked clergyman who undertakes to oppose himself to the mob bent upon killing Joe Christmas. That Hightower does not succeed is not important to Joe Christmas or to the reader. Christmas would have had to die, although not necessarily at the hands of lynchers. And in any event his death is not important. What Faulkner feels must be shown is the fact that at great risk, and fully aware of his danger, Hightower chooses sacrifice.

In *Soldier's Pay* the defection of Cecily is only one phase of the disillusionment that comes with peace after war. As defection it is less than nothing, since the man she is refusing to marry does not know or care anything about it. As evil, however, it must be opposed in the character of Emmy through her devotion to Donald, no matter what has happened to him, and through her stern independence toward Jones. Readers sometimes overlook Emmy because Faulkner has made Cecily more vivid, but Emmy is nevertheless there, and she is real.

At first glance it seems hard to find anything but rare tragedy in the figure of Nancy walking through the darkness toward her cabin, sure of death. And yet she does walk there. She does not try to run away. Throughout the story there is no moment at which Nancy tries to excuse herself. She would like not to die, but she has no doubt that she must. She can choose courage.

It may become apparent, then, that although Faulkner's horrors are horrible indeed, they have a moral value as well as that other value of dramatic demonstration. It is unfair, in view of Faulkner's stated purpose, to consider any one of his episodes isolated from its cause or effect or separated from its opposite. Horrors, when they occur (and they do not occur nearly as often as they are supposed) take their place as a part of those materials which convey Faulkner's purpose, and should be so regarded.

Pathos

No one, however, lives or would wish to live always at such a pitch of emotion as these situations involve. Faulkner's work would be beyond the endurance of any reader unless he could also write of people and situations in a state of more repose. Tragedy, even mere unhappy mood, appeals, but we do not accept repeatedly a plunge into an abyss of anguish. Humor is, in its way, a sign of wisdom; there is even satisfaction in being able simply to sit and look around, seeing the passing world but not being asked to pass judgment. Can Faulkner make us feel these qualities too? Can he give us pathos and humor and quiet good will? Certainly they are part of human experience, and to fail to show them would be to present less than the true picture of life. Perhaps the conflict in them is not intense, for much of living is not intense. But the conflict is there and may be demonstrated.

The danger in situations which stir sympathy is, of course, that the author may allow his emotions to trickle over into sentimentality, that he will ask his readers to feel pity in moments which cannot require it. Faulkner's handling of this problem is one of the most able parts of his fiction, and one to which critics have paid little attention, preoccupied as they have been with his more forceful evocations of terror and loathing.

Faulkner generally finds pathos in situations in which the characters are unconscious of the possibility of that situation's being any different or better than it is. They are unaware that there may even be a choice, and they see no reason for self-pity. Thus readers may be deeply moved by the opening chapter of *Light in August* in which Faulkner describes Lena's journey to Jefferson. She has walked all the way from Alabama; she is alone; she has very little time to wait before her child will be born among strangers. A reader imagining such a situation in his own life thinks of the difficulties of the journey, of the inevitable disappointment at the end. But none of this occurs to Lena. She has enjoyed the trip. People have been kind. She has no doubt of ultimate success. Geismar has called Lena an example of Faulkner's "single type of 'good' woman—a Southern madonna of low mentality."[70] Actually in her position her mentality or lack of it has nothing to do with the emotion she evokes. A reader may feel pity, but at the same time he knows his pity is unnecessary, since what seems pitiable to him does not seem so to Lena. Perhaps her mentality will not let her understand her life. Perhaps, however, she has simply a set of values by which she may accept difficult circumstances.

The same sort of pathos emerges from Cash's description of building the coffin in *As I Lay Dying*:

I made it on the bevel.
1. There is more surface for the nails to grip.
2. There is twice the gripping-surface to each seam.
3. The water will have to seep into it on a slant.
   Water moves easiest up or down or straight across.
4. In a house people are upright two-thirds of the time. So the seams and joints are made up-and-down. Because the stress is up-and-down.
5. In a bed where people lie down all the time, the joints and seams are made sideways, because the stress is sideways.
6. Except.
7. A body is not square like a cross-tie.
8. Animal magnetism.
9. The animal magnetism of a dead body makes the stress come slanting, so the seams and joints of a coffin are made on the bevel.
10. You can see by an old grave that the earth sinks down on the bevel.
11. While in a natural hole it sinks by the centre, the stress being up-and-down.
12. So I made it on the bevel.
13. It makes a neater job.[71]

Again, in "Pantaloon in Black" there is the pathos that comes with acceptance of the inevitable. The young colored man, unable to bear the death of his wife, deliberately provokes a fight, kills a white man, and dies for it. The story could be merely sensational, but Faulkner has deftly avoided this possibility by keeping us constantly aware of the love that was the cause of the action.

It (the lane) was empty at this hour of Sunday evening—no family in wagon, no rider, nor walkers churchward to speak to him and carefully refrain from looking after him when he had passed—the pale, powder-light, powder-dry dust of August from which the long week's marks of hoof and wheel had been blotted by the strolling and unhurried Sunday shoes, with somewhere beneath them, vanished but not gone, fixed and held in the annealing dust, the narrow, splay-toed prints of his wife's bare feet where on Saturday afternoons she would walk to the commissary to buy their next week's supplies while he took his bath; himself, his own prints, setting the period now as he strode on, moving almost as fast as a smaller man could have trotted, his body breasting the air her body had vacated, his eyes touching the objects—post and tree and field and house and hill—her eyes had lost.[72]

Rider never knew that there could be another way out. He could not kill himself, but he must die because he could not bear to live. Someone, therefore, must kill him, and to make that inevitable he must himself commit murder. Choosing as his victim a white man whose death would be a blessing, but who, because he is a white man, must not die unavenged, he goes through with his painfully thought-out plan.

Faulkner finds pathos, too, in situations in which a mistake carelessly and thoughtlessly made suddenly is seen to have hurt someone else. Here we are made to suffer for the victim but even more for the person whose words came out too quickly, and who must hereafter live with what he has done. In *Light in August* Byron Bunch tells Lena what he and we wish she might never need to know:

"What does he look like?" she says.
"Christmas? Why—"
"I don't mean Christmas."
"Oh. Brown. Yes. Tall, young. Dark complected; womenfolks call him handsome, a right smart do, I hear tell. A big hand for laughing and frolicking and playing jokes on folks. But I . . ." His voice ceases. He cannot look at her, feeling her steady, sober gaze upon his face.
"Joe Brown," she says. "Has he got a little white scar right by his mouth?"
And he cannot look at her, and he sits there on the stacked lumber when it is too late, and he could have bitten his tongue in two.[73]

And in "The Fire on the Hearth" a boy makes a mistake whose consequences are with him all his life:

Then one day the old curse of his fathers, the old haughty ancestral pride based not on any value but on an accident of geography, stemmed not from courage and honor but from wrong and shame, descended on him. He did not recognize it then. He and his foster brother, (a Negro) Henry, were just seven years old. They had finished supper at Henry's house and Molly was just sending them to bed in the room across the hall where they slept when there, when suddenly he said, "I'm going home."
"Les' stay here," Henry said. "I thought he was going toget up when pappy did and go hunting."
"You can," he said. He was already moving toward the door. "I'm going home."
"All right," Henry said, following him. And he remembered how they walked that half mile to his house in the first summer dark, himself walking just fast enough that the negro boy never quite came up beside him, entering the house in single file and up the stairs and into the room with the bed and the pallet on the floor which they slept on when they passed the night there, and how he undressed just slow enough for Henry to beat him to the pallet and lie down, and how he went to the bed and lay down on it, rigid, staring up at the dark ceiling even after he heard Henry raise onto one elbow, looking toward the bed with slow and equable astonishment. "Are you going to sleep up there?" Henry said. "Well, all right. This here pallet sleeps all right to me, but I reckon I just as lief to if you wants to," and rose

and approached the bed and stood over the white boy, waiting for him to move over and make room until the white boy said, harsh and violent though not out loud: "No!"

Henry didn't move. "You mean you don't want me to sleep in the bed?" Nor did the white boy move. He didn't answer, rigid on his back, staring upward. "All right," Henry said quietly and went back to the pallet and lay down again. . . . They did not hunt that morning. They never slept in the same room again and never ate at the same table because he admitted to himself it was shame now and he did not go to Henry's house and for a month he only saw Henry at a distance. . . . Then one day he knew it was grief and was ready to admit it was shame also, wanted to admit it only it was too late then, forever and forever too late. He went to Molly's house. It was already late afternoon; Henry and Lucas would be coming up from the field at any time now. Molly was there, looking at him from the kitchen door as he crossed the yard. There was nothing in her face; he said it the best he could for that moment, because later he would be able to say it right, say it once and forever so that it would be gone forever, facing her before he entered her house yet, stopping, his feet slightly apart, trembling a little, lordly, peremptory: "I'm going to eat supper with you all tonight."

It was all right. There was nothing in her face. He could say it almost any time now, when the time came. "Course you is," she said. "I'll cook you a chicken."

Then it was as if it had never happened at all. Henry came home almost at once; he must have seen him from the field, and he and Henry killed and dressed the chicken. Then Lucas came and he went to the barn with Henry and Lucas while Henry milked. Then they were busy in the yard in the dusk, smelling the cooking chicken, until Molly called Henry and then a little later himself, the voice as it had always been, peaceful and steadfast: "Come and eat your supper."

But it was too late. The table was set in the kitchen where it always was and Molly stood at the stove drawing the biscuit out as she always stood, but Lucas was not there and there was just one chair, one plate, his glass of milk beside it, the platter heaped with untouched chicken, and even as he sprang back, gasping, for an instant blind as the room rushed and swam, Henry was turning toward the door to go out of it.

"Are you ashamed to eat when I eat?" he cried.

Henry paused, turning his head a little to speak in the voice slow and without heat: "I aint shamed of nobody," he said peacefully. "Not even me."[74]

Repose

Often, however, Faulkner is not asking his readers to do anything more than enjoy themselves as the story moves slowly along. Nothing is at stake in "The Bear" when young Ike McCaslin rides to Memphis with old Boon, at least nothing of which Ike is aware. He is enjoying the adventures of the trip, the things he sees along the track through the logging preserve, and the sights and sounds of the city. Bayard Sartoris may have his own problems on his mind during his visit to the McCallums, but they know nothing of his mental torment, and readers watching them are inclined to forget it too. Nothing happens for many pages in "The Bear" and "Delta Autumn" while Faulkner describes to his readers the forest country. And in "The Courthouse" and "The Jail" we are submerged in history filled with great events which have been leveled and dwarfed by time so that the impact they make is merely small and pleasant. These moments of repose are frequent in Faulkner's work. They are opportunities to turn our eyes away for a moment from the characters and the problems which have been engrossing us and to rest our eyes and our thoughts on objects and ideas smaller and more distant:

> As they approached, the groaning and creaking of the mill would be the first intimation, unless the wind happened to blow toward them; then it would be the sharp, subtly exciting odor of fermentation and of boiling molasses. Bayard liked the smell of it and they would drive up and stop for a time while the boy rolled his eyes covertly at them as he fed cane into the mill, while they watched the patient mule and the old man stooped over the simmering pot. Sometimes Bayard got out and went over and talked to him, leaving Narcissa in the car, lapped in the ripe odors of the falling year and all its rich, vague sadness, her gaze brooding on Bayard and the old negro—the one lean and tall and fatally young and the other stooped with time, and her spirit went out in serene and steady waves, surrounding him unawares.
>
> Then he would return and get in beside her and she would touch his rough clothing, but so lightly that he was not conscious of it, and they would drive back along the faint, uneven road, beside the flaunting woods, and soon, above turning locusts and oaks, the white house, simple and huge and steadfast, and the orange disc of the harvest moon above the ultimate hills, as ripe as cheese.[75]

Humor

If the "harmonized, balanced view of human existence" includes struggle and repose, it must also have in it much of the saving grace of humor. Critics have noticed that Faulkner is humorous but, to their minds, dubiously so. In discussing Faulkner's humor, one critic has called it "curious, unsmiling humor at remote control,"[76] and another describes it as "derived from the frontier tradition."[77] Snell has given it four characteristics: "sardonic and abrasive," showing "little human sympathy," the "hard laughter of cruelty and satire," and the "obverse of the saturnine melancholy which underlies all Faulkner's work."[78]

What one man will laugh at is any other man's guess, but it is hard not to smile, at least, any number of times in Faulkner's stories. The humor does not lie in the words themselves, but in the characters and the situations in which they are involved. Sometimes it is a question of men angrily entangled in a hopeless and ridiculous impasse out of which they must sheepishly find their way. This is what happens in "The Courthouse" when the lock for the United States mailbag is lost after it has been taken off the mailbag and used to embellish an impromptu jail. The resulting search with amused Indians looking on, the harried discussions about what to do, and the triumphant solution which results in the formation of the town are described with deliberate understatement, while the reader enjoys the knowledge that the situation is not impossible and that the people involved are doing the best they can in the mood of men about to pay their income taxes. But the heart of the humor is that a group of men used to having their own way are forced to knuckle under to a "frail irascible little man weighing less than a hundred pounds" who "will ride six hundred miles through this country every two weeks with nothing for protection but a foxhorn" and who "aint really interested in confusion any more than he is in money"—but who just happens to be in that place the representative of the United States of America.

Faulkner often finds amusement in the sight of someone's getting what he deserves. In "A Courtship" two strong and arrogant young men ply themselves with increasingly impossible tasks to prove the right of one of them to the most eligible young lady of the Indian community, while the maiden is quietly but firmly spirited away by a third young man who cannot be bothered to move a muscle in his own behalf. In a wonderful tale of horse-trading in *The Hamlet* it is fascinating to watch while two experts at the business work on each other, one because he intends to get something for nothing if he can, the other because he would rather trade horses than eat. In the end justice is done, and pleasure in reading is the result.

In the story memorably entitled "My Grandmother Millard and General Bedford Forrest and the Battle of Harrykin Creek" a series of fantastic and hilarious events result fron an old lady's worthy purpose of saving the family silver from Yankee soldiers. Except for her error in judgment of their chivalry everything would undoubtedly have gone well, but unfortunately the scheme does not work out just as planned.

Much of Faulkner's most affectionate amusement is reserved for the mules and hound dogs which are among his most important characters, and one of his best passages describes the mule with understanding and respect:

Round and round the mule went, setting its narrow deerlike feet delicately down in the hissing canepith, its neck bobbing limber as a section of rubber hose in the collar, with its trace-galled flanks and flopping, lifeless ears, and its half-closed eyes drowsing venomously behind pale lids, apparently asleep with the monotony of its own motion. Some Homer of the cotton fields should sing the saga of the mule and of his place in the South. He it was more than any other one creature or thing who, steadfast to the land when all else faltered before the hopeless juggernaut of circumstances, impervious to conditions that broke man's hearts because of his venomous and patient preoccupation with the immediate present, won the prone South from beneath the iron heel of Reconstruction and taught it pride again through humility, and courage through adversity overcome; who accomplished the well-nigh impossible despite hopeless odds, by sheer and vindictive patience. Father and mother he does not resemble, sons and daughters he will never have; vindictive and patient (it is a known fact that he will labor ten years willingly and patiently for you, for the privilege of kicking you once); solitary but without pride, self-sufficient but without vanity; his voice is his own derision. Outcast and pariah, he has neither friend, wife, mistress, or sweetheart; celibate, he is unscarred, possesses neither pillar nor desert cave, he is not assaulted by temptations nor flagellated by dreams nor assuaged by vision; faith, hope and charity are not his. Misanthropic, he labors six days without reward for one creature whom he hates, bound with chains to another whom he despises, and spends the seventh day kicking or being kicked by his fellows. Misunderstood even by that creature, the nigger who drives him, whose impulses and mental processes most closely resemble his, he performs alien actions in alien surroundings; he finds bread not only for a race, but for an entire form of behavior; meek, his inheritance is cooked away from him along with his soul in a glue factory. Ugly, untiring and perverse, he can be moved neither by reason, flattery, nor promise of reward; he performs his humble monotonous duties without complaint, and his meed is blows. Alive he is haled through the world, an object of general derision; unwept, unhonored and unsung, he bleaches his awkward bones among rusting cans and broken crockery and worn-out automobile tires on lonely hillsides while his flesh soars unawares against the blue in craws of buzzards.[79]

Another short paragraph gives an unforgettable picture of a frightened puppy on its first hunting trip:

There was a scurrying noise in the leaves behind them and a tense whimpering, and the young dog came into the light and slid with squeaking whimpers, and the diffident, fleeting phosphorus of its eyes against Caspey's leg. "Whut you want?" Caspey said, dropping his hand on its head. "Somethin' skeer you out dar?" The puppy genuflected its gawky young body and nuzzled whimpering at Caspey's hand. "He mus' 'a' foun' a bear down yonder," Caspey said. "Wouldn't dem other dawgs he'p you ketch 'im?"

"Poor little fellow," Narcissa said. "Did he really get scared, Caspey? Come here, puppy."

"De other dawgs jes' went off and lef' 'im," Caspey answered. The puppy moiled diffidently about Caspey's knees. Then it scrambled up and licked his face.[80]

Readers may object that such passages do not seem particularly amusing, and out of context they do not. Faulkner's humor arises naturally from his characters and situations and has little impact apart from them. It is important to notice humor in his work, however, since it has a forceful part to play in the development of his idea of the truths of the human heart. His characters never set out to be funny. There is no purposely brilliant repartee. But the unconsciously amusing things the characters do and say are part of their inmost natures. The account of the puppy pleases because not only does it tell us about the puppy himself; it gives a little more information about Caspey. The same thing is true of the incident which closes *Intruder in the Dust* (Lucas has asked Gavin Stevens for his bill for legal services):

'Two dollars?' Lucas said. He blinked again. Then he blinked twice again. 'Just two dollars?' Now he just blinked once then he did something with his breath: not a sigh, simply a discharge of it, putting his first two fingers into the purse: 'That don't sound like much to me but then I'm a farming man and you're a lawing man and whether you know your business or not I reckon it aint none of my red wagon as the music box says to try to learn you different:' and drew from the purse a worn bill crumpled into a ball not much larger than a shriveled olive and opened it out enough to read it then opened it out and laid it on the desk and from the purse took a half dollar and laid it on the desk then counted onto the desk from the purse one by one four dimes and two nickels and then counted them again with his forefinger, moving them one by one about half an inch, his lips moving under the moustache, the purse still open in the other hand, then he picked up two of the dimes and a nickel and put them into the hand holding the open purse and took from the purse a quarter and put it on the desk and looked down at the coins for a rapid second then put the two dimes and the nickel back on the desk and took up the half dollar and put it back into the purse.

'That aint but six bits,' his uncle said.

'Nemmine that,' Lucas said and took up the quarter and dropped it back into the purse and closed it and watching Lucas he realised that the purse had at least two different compartments and maybe more, a second almost elbow-deep section opening beneath Lucas' fingers and for a time Lucas stood looking down into it exactly as you would look down at your reflection in a well then took from that compartment a knotted soiled cloth tobacco sack bulging and solid looking which struck on the desk top with a dull thick chink.

'That makes it out,' he said. 'Four bits in pennies. I was aiming to take them to the bank but you can save me the trip. You want to count 'um?'

'Yes,' his uncle said. 'But you're the one paying the money. You're the one to count them.'

'It's fifty of them,' Lucas said.

'This is business,' his uncle said. So Lucas unknotted the sack and dumped the pennies out on the desk and counted them one by one moving each one with his forefinger into the first small mass of dimes and nickels, counting aloud, then snapped the purse shut and put it back inside his coat and with the other hand shoved the whole mass of coins and the crumpled bill across the table until the desk blotter stopped them and took a bandana handkerchief from the side pocket of the coat and wiped his hands and put the handkerchief back and stood again intractable and calm and not looking at either of them now while the fixed blaring of the radios and the blatting creep of the automobile horns and all the rest of the whole County's Saturday uproar came up on the bright afternoon.

'Now what?' his uncle said. 'What are you waiting for now?'

'My receipt,' said Lucas.[81]

The incident seems ridiculous and out of its context it may make little sense. To one who knows the kind of person Lucas is and what has happened to him in the story, as well as the purpose of the uncle's two dollar charge, the whole scene is a monumental and well-deserved victory for Lucas.

Far from finding Faulkner's humor unsympathetic, sardonic, or satiric, it seems possible to argue that the laughter it brings is more likely to be kindly and warm. That is Faulkner's own attitude toward his characters, and many of his readers have the same feeling. They may find any of the characters funny sometimes, but there is no character who is present in a book just to supply a laugh. None is a caricature. Faulkner is not trying to make his people ridiculous, and they never are. They may be in what a reader would call a ridiculous situation, until he remembers that what is ridiculous in life is the thing that is happening to someone else. Faulkner's characters, in their own eyes, are trying to solve immediate problems the best way they can. They are not thinking of their own entertainment value. There is a propriety, a lack of exaggeration in Faulkner's use of humor that many readers find significant to their full understanding of the characters and their stories. It adds a dimension and helps to clarify what the same characters may do in a more serious situation.

Nature

Another aspect of the view of human experience to be considered in assessing Faulkner's work is his understanding of nature. Miss Drew in *The Modern Novel* sets certain standards to be met by literature with a "background of countryside."[82] These may well be applied to Faulkner's work since Yoknapatawpha county depends for its living upon what it can produce in its fields and forests. A good novel of the soil, Miss Drew maintains, needs more than keenness of observation of nature and people and delicacy of description.[83] It is "not a mere statement of elemental truths about immutable earth and the essential reality of peasant life."[84] The earth and the people must both be felt strongly enough to "fuse them so that the story cannot be thought of out of its setting."[85] The story itself must be "created from earth not constructed against the background of a certain locality."[86] It must have interest and gain intensity in the setting which helps produce the sense of truth about human character.

Certainly Faulkner is a keen observer of nature, as he is of people, and his expression of his observation is often poetic and lyrical:

But Sam wouldn't come out. They would leave him there. He would come as far as the road where the surrey waited, to take the riding horses back, and that was all. The men would ride the horses and Uncle Ash and Tennie's Jim and the boy would follow in the wagon with Sam, with the camp equipment and the trophies, the meat, the heads, the antlers, the good ones, the wagon winding on among the tremendous gums and cypresses and oaks where no axe save that of the hunter had ever sounded, between the impenetrable walls of cane and brier—the two changing yet constant walls just beyond which the wilderness whose mark he had brought away forever on his spirit even from that first two weeks seemed to lean, stooping a little, watching them and listening, not quite inimical because they were too small, even those such as Walter and Major de Spain and old General Compson who had killed many deer and bear, their sojourn too brief and too harmless to excite to that, but just brooding, secret, tremendous, almost inattentive.

Then they would emerge, they would be out of it, the line as sharp as the demarcation of a doored wall. Suddenly skeleton cotton- and corn-fields would flow away on either hand, gaunt and motionless beneath the gray rain; there would be a house, barns, fences, where the hand of man had clawed for an instant, holding, the wall of the wilderness behind them now, tremendous and still and seemingly impenetrable in the gray and fading light, the very tiny orifice through which they had emerged apparently swallowed up.[87]

Faulkner sees nature, however, as more than the background against which his characters live out their lives. To his mind, Warren says nature is a moral force, almost another character. The relationship of man to nature is an indication of the relationship of man to man, and is equally important. Those who have not the right feeling for it are "truly evil men."[88] Nature cannot be owned,[89] and those who seek to exploit it never really have anything, although they may gain possession and use it for a little while. Those who denude forests, who impoverish the soil, who seek to use nature for gain are the real criminals. Their "desire for power over nature goes with their lust for power over man," and their crimes against nature, like their crimes against man are always avenged."[90]

This Delta, he thought: This Delta. This land which man has deswamped and denuded and derivered in two generations so that white men can own plantations and commute every night to Memphis and black men can own plantations and ride in jim crow cars to Chicago to live in millionaires' mansions on Lake Shore Drive, where white men can rent farms and live like niggers and niggers crop on shares and live like animals, where cotton is planted and grows man-tall in the very cracks of the sidewalks, and usury and mortgage and bankruptcy and measureless wealth, Chinese and African and Aryan and Jew, all breed and spawn togther until no man has time to say which one is which nor cares. . . . No wonder the ruined woods I used to know don't cry for retribution! he thought: The people who have destroyed it will accomplish its revenge.[91]

The thesis that nature cannot be owned is the theme of "The Bear" and *Absalom, Absalom!* and of the story of the Snopeses. When Ike McCaslin with Sam Fathers to help him finally learns that he does not want power over the bear, he realizes also that he does not want power over the land. He no longer wants to own it; indeed he knows that he should not own it. That realization never comes to Thomas Sutpen. He thinks that he can acquire land and with it power over his fellows. The War destroys his land, and one of the least of the men he had owned destroys him. The Snopeses have beggared their land. They farm one tract till it is exhausted and then move on, on an endless journey, during which they earn for themselves nothing but the hatred of their neighbors.

Nature is not Faulkner's god. It is not a blind, implacable force. It seems to be rather an opportunity which a man may use or misuse. What he does indicates what he is likely to do about his fellowmen. The two attitudes are indistinguishable.

A mile back he had left the rich, broad, flat river-bottom country and entered the hills—a region which topographically was the final blue and dying echo of the Appalachian mountains. Chickasaw Indians had owned it, but after the Indians it had been cleared where possible for cultivation, and after the Civil War, forgotten save by the small peripatetic sawmills which had vanished too now, their sites marked only by the mounds of rotting sawdust which were not only their gravestones but the monuments of a people's heedless greed.[92]

Religion

In concluding the discussion of Faulkner's view of life as it is revealed in his work, we need to consider his place in relation to one of the noticeable trends in modern writing. Probably as a result of the War and of the uncertainties which have followed it many readers are seeking a religious meaning in their fiction. Writers of all faiths are making frank appeal to popular taste—as is apparent in the work of Graham Green, Lloyd Douglas, and Jessamyn West. More esoteric readers have found pleasure in the posthumous novels of Charles Williams and in the poetry of the Anglo-Catholic T. S. Eliot. Religion has discovered that fiction furnishes an excellent medium for its teachings, and readers have found in such novels a source of inspiration.

Critics have never credited Faulkner with any religious convictions; indeed they have made him sound almost like an arch-foe of all belief in God. Hartwick says that his books lack "spiritual resonance";[93] Millett finds him writing like a "man possessed of devils";[94] Luccock feels that Faulkner's work is paralleled by the "movement in theology expressing the sense of the malignant evil of life."[95] Geismar believes that much of Faulkner's work must be placed in the "tradition of reversionary, neo-pagan neurotic discontent which also produced Fascism."[96] On the other side the editors of the newly-founded *Faulkner Studies* in the general introduction to their publication say that today's stress is upon the "brilliant sociological import of the work" (Faulkner's) but make no mention of spiritual values.[97]

Neither interpretation seems to be upheld by statements in Faulkner's two addresses, the first from his Nobel prize acceptance speech:

He (man) is immortal not because he alone among creatures has an inexhaustible voice, but because he has a soul, a spirit capable of compassion and endurance.[98]

The second is found in his talk to the graduating class:

It is not man in the mass who can and will save Man. It is Man himself, created in the image of God so that he shall have the power and the will to choose right from wrong, and so be able to save himself because he is worth saving;[99]

These are not the words of a pessimist, nor are they the words of a sociologist. They appear to be the words of a man who has a profound and optimistic belief in Man himself, failing possibly, but failing through his own fault, not because he is the victim of a malignant fate or of unfavorable circumstances.

These, however, are words which were spoken in public and upon inspirational occasions. Some readers may be cynical enough to wonder just how much they are echoed in Faulkner's writing, especially since no critic has ever emphasized such ideas. What belief, if any, does Faulkner actually express?

Although Faulkner never gives us any religious ideas through author comment, the ethical choices with which he presents his characters are essentially Christian ones—between justice and injustice, courage and cowardice, sacrifice and greed, pity and self. In his attitude toward his characters, Faulkner also demonstrates that those whom he admires are those who exert compassion, courage, and the proper kind of pride: Ratliff, Miss Habersham, Sam Fathers. Toward characters whose actions range from the unethical to frankly criminal Faulkner always shows understanding. He is careful to point out in every case the circumstances which aggravated an original flaw. The facts of Joe Christmas's birth, the incident of the toothpaste, his life with the Mc-

Eacherns all help to explain his career. When we understand some of the frustrations of their lives it is easy to understand why the Snopeses should be envious of their neighbors and why Thomas Sutpen became obsessed with his dream of power. Faulkner does not spare these characters; neither does he condemn them without a hearing. His people are seldom hopeless of redemption, although it does not always happen, and when it does it may be in a peculiar way. Some of Faulkner's readers have been chilled by the redemption of Temple Drake implied in *Requiem for a Nun,* since that redemption is brought about by a murder. It seems possible to argue, however, that Temple's need was desperate and that the only way to save her was by such a demonstration of faith as Nancy's. A less remarkable but no less convincing bit of evidence of Faulkner's faith in human possibility is the purchase of the toy cow by one of the Snopeses (the only member of that clan who shows a trace of normal kindness). After he has, at Ratliff's insistence, bought and disposed of the cow with which his idiot relative was in love, he replaces it with the cheap toy—not, perhaps, an indication of much generosity, but an important step for a Snopes.

If Faulkner is unsparing in his portrayal of human depravity in such characters as Popeye and the Snopeses, he is equally unsparing in his insistence that man has, if he wishes, the opportunity to save himself. In *Intruder in the Dust* Gavin Stevens and his nephew discuss that problem:

'So man is always right,' he said.
'No,' his uncle said. 'He tries to be if they who use him for their own power and aggrandisement let him alone. Pity and justice and conscience too—that belief in more than the divinity of individual man (which we in America have debased into a national religion of the entrails in which man owes no duty to his soul because he has been absolved of a soul to owe duty to and instead is static heir at birth to an inevictable quit-claim on a wife a car a radio and an old-age pension) but in the divinity of his continuity as Man.[100]

Again the opportunity is offered in this passage in *Sartoris:*

The negroes drank with him, amicably, a little diffidently—two opposed concepts, antipathetic by race, blood, nature and environment, touching for a moment and fused within an illusion—human-kind forgetting its lust and cowardice and greed for a day. "Chris'mus," the woman murmured shyly. "Thanky, suh."[101]

In *Soldiers' Pay* one of the characters is the clergyman father of the hopelessly disfigured and dying Donald Mahon. After Donald's death his father and Gilligan have this conversation:

"Circumstance moves in marvellous ways, Joe."
"I thought you'd a said God, reverend."
"God is circumstance, Joe. God is in this life. We know nothing about the next. That will take care of itself in good time. 'The Kingdom of God is in a man's heart,' the Book says."
"Ain't that a kind of funny doctrine for a parson to get off?"
"Remember, I am an old man, Joe. Too old for bickering or bitterness. We make

our own heaven or hell in this world. Who knows; perhaps when we die we may not be required to go anywhere or do anything at all. That would be heaven."[102]

In two passages, one in "The Old People" and one in *The Wild Palms*, Faulkner makes a point which seems important to him: it is better to have grief than to have nothing, since grief is a part of life. In the short story Ike and his cousin are talking about the ghostly deer they have each seen following their first kill:

"Think of all that has happened here, on this earth. All the blood hot and strong for living, pleasuring, that has soaked back into it. For grieving and suffering too, of course, but still getting something out of it for all that, getting a lot out of it, because after all you don't have to continue to bear what you believe is suffering; you can always choose to stop that, put an end to that. And even suffering and grieving is better than nothing; there is only one thing worse than not being alive, and that's shame. But you can't be alive forever, and you always wear out life long before you have exhausted the possibilities of living. And all that must be somewhere; all that could not have been invented and created just to be thrown away. And the earth is shallow; there is not a great deal of it before you come to the rock. And the earth don't want to keep things, hoard them; it wants to use them again. Look at the seed, the acorns, at what happens even to carrion when you try to bury it: it refuses too, seethes and struggles too until it reaches light and air again, hunting the sun still.[103]

The young doctor in *The Wild Palms* has just thrown away the poison with which he might have avoided the consequences of his own mistake:

So it is the old meat after all, no matter how old. Because if memory exists outside of the flesh it won't be memory because it won't know what it remembers so when she became not then half of memory became not and if I become not then all of remembering will cease to be—Yes, he thought, between grief and nothing I will take grief.[104]

If Faulkner shows no interest in most orthodox forms of religious expression he has only respect for the Negroes and their church. One of the memorable passages in *Sound and Fury* describes a service to which Dilsey and her family take Benny. The scene is described with loving care and without a hint of supercilious amusement.[105] And in *Soldiers' Pay*, Faulkner gives us this picture of the Negro church:

The singing drew nearer and nearer; at last, crouching among a clump of trees beside the road, they saw the shabby church with its canting travesty of a spire. Within it was a soft glow of kerosene serving only to make the darkness and the heat thicker, making thicker the imminence of sex after harsh labor along the mooned land; and from it welled the crooning submerged passion of the dark race. It was nothing, it was everything; then it swelled to an ecstasy, taking the white man's words as readily as it took his remote God and made a personal Father of Him.
Feed Thy Sheep, O Jesus. All the longing of mankind for a Oneness with Something, somewhere. Feed Thy Sheep, O Jesus. . . .[106]

These do not seem to be the words of a writer who himself lacks belief and scorns the beliefs of others. They seem rather to express the idea and attitude of a person poignantly aware of man's deep spiritual need. It is worth noting here that Breit has seen a similarity between

Faulkner and El Greco.[107] It is possible to argue that this is based chiefly on the fact that both are aware of the value of distortion, but it is equally possible that the novelist and the painter are alike moved by pity to attempt to express the almost inexpressible yearning for spiritual satisfaction in the heart of mankind.

FAULKNER'S CHARACTERS

Presentation

It may be noted that in this discussion of Faulkner's work there has been constant emphasis upon the relation of his method to his characters. When we think of the work of any great novelist and of the satisfactions in rereading a certain book, we frequently wish to meet the characters again. We can forget the sequence of events in *Pride and Prejudice,* for example, but we can never forget the personality of Elizabeth Bennett. We may not remember all that happened in *Return of the Native* but we never lose our recollection of the characters, even if their names escape us. We can describe Becky Sharp as a woman long after we have forgotten what she did.

It is important, then, as we read Faulkner to pay close attention to the characters he gives us and to see why they may remain memorable as individuals when what happens to them is long forgotten. With Faulkner we have also the problem of considering his characters in the light of the criticism we have already mentioned. If Faulkner has been fair with his readers in his presentation of life, has appealed to all the emotions which are a part of normal human experience, and still has given us characters who are incredible or whom we do not care to remember, his achievement is ephemeral. And who would wish to recall an author's characters if they were superficially created:

They (Faulkner's characters) live, they live copiously and brilliantly; but they live by the violence with which Faulkner sustains them, by the sullen, screaming intensity which he breathes into them (often with Faulkner's own gestures, fury, and raging confusion of pronouns) by the atmospheric terror which encloses them. They live because they are incredibilities in action, because they have been scoured by death before they reach the grave, so that one sees them always in the posture of some frantic relinquishment and irrevocable agony, the body taut and the soul quivering in death.[108]

These are harsh words, but they express the impression which many reputable critics have of Faulkner's characterization and which discourages investigation of his work. It is well to know that such an attack has been made and to consider it a strong reason for a thorough study of what Faulkner has actually done.

We know that Faulkner uses as characters the citizens of Yoknapatawpha county: all ages, sizes, shades, and intelligence quotients. Some of them are now dead, but their personalities are well known to their descendants and to us. We know their moral standards or lack of them, their economic prosperity or lack of it, and their ability or inability to get along with their fellowmen. If we are sure of one thing it is that it would be impossible to make any statement that would cover more than a few of them, unless it might be that at some time each was resident in Yoknapatawpha county, Mississippi.

While much of what we know of these people is discovered through ~~Faulkner's~~ what they say and do, we are indebted for our first impressions of them ~~Descriptions~~ to Faulkner's descriptions. These are reminiscent of Chaucer in their emphasis upon important details not only of appearance but also of personality and habits, and in their careful selection and arrangement. Sometimes they seem incomplete: we may not know how tall or how old or how intelligent an individual is; but that is because at that moment that information is not needed. If it ever is, it will be given, but otherwise it does not clutter up our thinking. This, for example, is our introduction to Joe Christmas:

And the group of men in the planer shed looked up and saw the stranger standing there, watching them. They did not know how long he had been there. He looked like a tramp, yet not like a tramp either. His shoes were dusty and his trousers were soiled too. But they were of decent serge, sharply creased, and his shirt was soiled but it was a white shirt, and he wore a tie and a stiff-brim straw hat that was quite new, cocked at an angle arrogant and baleful above his still face. He did not look like a professional hobo in his professional rags, but there was something definitely rootless about him, as though no town nor city was his, no street, no walls, no square inch of earth his home. And that he carried his knowledge with him always as though it were a banner, with a quality ruthless, lonely, and almost proud. "As if," the men said later, "he was just down on his luck for a time, and that he didn't intend to stay down on it and didn't give a damn much how he rose up." He was young. And Byron watched him standing there and looking at the men in sweatstained overalls, with a cigarette in one side of his mouth and his face darkly and contemptuously still, drawn down a little on one side because of the smoke. After a while he spat the cigarette without touching his hand to it and turned and went on to the mill office while the men in faded and worksoiled overalls looked at his back with a sort of baffled outrage.[109]

Faulkner uses the same painstaking methods in describing characters who may appear only for a moment:

Now not only Varner but all the others looked at the speaker—a gaunt man in absolutely clean though faded and patched overalls and even freshly shaven, with a gentle, almost sad face until you unravelled what were actually two separate expressions—a temporary one of static peace and quiet overlaying a constant one of definite even though faint harriedness, and a sensitive mouth which had a quality of adolescent freshness and bloom until you realised that this could just as well be the result of a lifelong abstinence from tobacco—the face of a breathing archetype and protagonist of all men who marry young and father only daughters and are themselves but the eldest daughter of their own wives. His name was Tull.[110]

Some of Faulkner's first descriptions are lavished on the Snopeses. This is the Hamlet's first glimpse of Flem:

He rode up on a gaunt mule, on a saddle which was recognizable at once as belonging to the Varners, with a tin pail tied to it. He hitched the mule to a tree behind the store and untied the pail and came and mounted to the gallery, where already a dozen men, Ratliff among them, lounged. He did not speak. If he ever looked at them individually, that one did not discern it—a thick squat soft man of no establishable age between twenty and thirty, with a broad still face containing a tight seam of mouth stained slightly at the corners with tobacco, and eyes the color of stagnant water, and projecting from among the other features in startling and sudden paradox, a tiny predatory nose like the beak of a small hawk. It was as though the original nose had been left off by the original designer or craftsman and the unfinished job taken over by someone of a radically different school or perhaps by some viciously maniacal humorist or perhaps by one who had only time to clap into the center of the face a frantic and desperate warning.[111]

Sometimes the description is given as one character recalls another:

Nancy would set the bundle on the top of her head, then upon the bundle in turn she would set the black straw sailor hat which she wore winter and summer. She was tall, with a high, sad face, sunken a little where her teeth were missing. Sometimes we would go a part of the way down the lane and across the pasture with her to watch the balanced bundle and the hat that never bobbed or wavered, even when she walked down into the ditch and up on the other side and stooped through the fence. She would go down on her hands and knees and crawl through the gap, her head rigid, up tilted, the bundle steady as a rock or a balloon, and rise to her feet again and go on.[112]

Often descriptive details are repeated from story to story. Thomas Sutpen's French architect first appears in *Absalom, Absalom!*

. . . two months later he returned, again without warning and accompanied this time by the covered wagon with a negro driving it and on the seat with the negro a small alertly resigned man with a grim, harried Latin face, in a frock coat and a flowered waistcoat and a hat which would have created no furore on a Paris boulevard, all of which he was to wear constantly for the next two years—the sombrely theatric clothing and the expression of fatalistic and amazed determination—while his white client and the negro crew which he was to advise though not direct went stark naked save for a coating of dried mud.[113]

In "The Courthouse" almost the same description is given of the same man:

. . . He had even brought with him a tame Parisian architect—or captive rather, since it was said in Ratcliffe's back room that the man slept at night in a kind of pit at the side of the chateau he was planning, tied wrist to wrist with one of his captor's Carib slaves; indeed the settlement had only to see him once to know that he was no dociler than his captor, any more than the weasel or rattlesnake is no less untame than the wolf or the bear before which it gives way until completely and hopelessly cornered: a man no larger than Pettigrew, with humor—our sardonic undefeated eyes which had seen everything and believed none of it, in the broad expansive hat and brocaded waistcoat and ruffled wrists of a half-artist, half-boulevardier; and they—Compson perhaps, Peabody certainly—could imagine him in his mud-stained brier-slashed brocade and lace standing in a trackless wilderness dreaming colonnades and porticoes and fountains and promenades in the style of David, with just behind each elbow an identical giant half-naked Negro not even watching him, only breathing, moving each time he took a step or shifted like his shadow repeated in two and blown to gigantic size.[114]

Types

Like any other author Faulkner is temperamentally fitted to deal expertly with certain types of personality and less able to handle others.

Just as it would be impossible to imagine Henry James and Hardy adopting each other's characters or to guess what George Eliot would do with the foremost hands of the *Narcissus*, so we must realize that *Natural limitations* Faulkner has his natural limitations. Thus he never seems to make a reality of women unless they are what has been called "Southern madonnas of low mentality" or stubbornly old and tough like Miss Habersham or Aunt Jenny or Negroes like Molly and Dilsey and Nancy. Temple Drake in *Sanctuary*, Cecily Saunders in *Soldiers' Pay*, and Belle Middleton in *Sartoris* never seem to come off: possibly because they are the sort of people they are, Faulknerian versions of the flapper, skinny, brainless, and oversexed. It is a type which has not appeared in his more recent work. They probably have no appeal to Faulkner, and consequently none to his readers, because it is impossible to imagine such women facing with any compassion or courage a choice between good and evil.

But when Faulkner is free of these troublesome females and their satellite men he is enormously successful. His other characters are the ones who would normally live in a place like Yoknapatawpha county, and the county is the sort of place Faulkner himself has lived in all his life. He has always been familiar with the ways of Negroes and poor whites and an impoverished Southern aristocracy. He is an old friend of mules and hounds and fyces; he is well aware of what they will do under almost any circumstances. This knowledge and understanding are poured into his writing with such a lavish hand that it is almost impossible to understand the critic who said, "Faulkner's characters would be more effective if they were contrasted with normal characters."[115]

Although Faulkner certainly does not blink at the necessity of showing his readers people of low mentality or low morality—people like Joe Christmas or Popeye or the tribe of Snopes—and does not seek to hide their bad qualities, the depth of his analysis always explains their defects and earns some sympathy for them. He must show these characters in their entirety, but when he is able to turn from them to show his readers the other side of the picture, he makes the good as real as he has made the bad. His old women—Aunt Jenny, Miss Habersham, Mrs. Littlejohn—are warmly drawn and happily convincing. They rule those around them with goodhumored firmness, acid in their speech but kindly in their intent. Their responsibilities include their menfolk, servants, young relatives, and animals, toward all of whom they exhibit a disillusioned patience which Faulkner treats with respectful amusement.

"Simon says fiddlesticks," Miss Jenny snapped. "Have you lived with Simon sixty years without learning that he don't know the truth when he sees it?" And she followed Simon from the room and on to the kitchen, and while Simon's tall yellow daughter bent over her biscuit board and Simon filled a glass pitcher with fresh water and sliced lemons and set them and a sugar bowl and two tall glasses on a tray, Miss Jenny stood in the doorway and curled Simon's grizzled remaining hair into tighter kinks yet. She had a fine command of language at all times, but when her ire was aroused she soared without effort to sublime heights. Hers was a forceful clarity and a colorful simplicity that Demosthenes would have envied and which even mules comprehended and of whose intent the most obtuse persons remained not long in doubt; and beneath it Simon's head bobbed lower and lower and the fine assumption of detached preoccupation moulted like feathers from about him, until he caught up the tray and ducked from the room.[116]

More than half the population of Yoknapatawpha county is Negro, and in his development of these characters Faulkner is at his best. They are not the Negroes of the North, educated and independent. They have grown up in the county, and, with the exception of a few like Caspey, who went away to war and on the way acquired a few unwelcome ideas, they have known no other surroundings. Some of them are the children of slaves and all of them have slave ancestors. Many of them have no concept of life except the one they lead in Yoknapatawpha, and most of them would be lost without the white folks who employ them.

Among critics Faulkner's treatment of his negro characters has led to considerable comment. Cowley believes that the author thinks of them as an element of stability and endurance in the county, with the octoroons forming the element of instability.[117] Warren thinks that Faulkner sees the Negro as a "reminder of the guilt of slavery,"[118] a sort of racial hair shirt. Geismar believes that Faulkner feels that the emancipated Negro is the cause of the destruction of all that Faulkner himself holds dear, and that by showing him as "inhuman, criminal, degenerate," Faulkner "proclaims his anger."[119]

It is difficult, however, to find the evidences Geismar has found of Faulkner's anger. Negroes appear in many of the stories, as they could hardly fail to do in any story of Mississippi. With the exception of Joe Christmas there is no criminal among them, and many readers find him less criminal than the men who take the law into their hands against him. It would be difficult to find anything "criminal, degenerate, or inhuman" in Dilsey, who manages somehow to keep life functioning in the feckless Compson household, or in Lucas Beauchamp, a half-breed whose white blood is asserted not by an attempt to rebel but by the firm insistence upon certain forms of speech. These strengthen his own self respect because he knows that they are fully understood and appreciated by his friends and neighbors, both white and colored.

Certainly Faulkner feels no anger toward Nancy, whose desperate measure brings Temple Stevens to the realization of her own duty. Nancy did what she did because "I tried everything I knowed."[120] Having committed murder she has no hesitation about dying for it. She is a proud and moving figure, hardly a reminder of guilt or the object of anger.

It seems possible to argue that if Faulkner feels anything more than a general interest in the Negroes (and, of course, he does) it is a respectful admiration for the qualities which have helped them endure not only the shame of slavery but the perils of reconstruction. In the course of time they and the whites have learned to live together in peace and harmony, and the only thing that threatens that peace is the earnest efforts of do-gooders to hasten the day of racial equality. Faulkner is not against racial equality; but he does oppose its imposition from outside, not upon one race which is not ready for it but upon two which are unprepared.

'I only say that the injustice is ours, the South's. We must expiate and abolish it ourselves, alone and without help nor even (with thanks) advice.'[121]

He seems to feel, if such characters as Nancy and Dilsey and Molly Beauchamp can be believed, that white people have much to learn from the Negroes of the human values he considers important. He portrays the Negro's ability to adjust to circumstances:

One day even I realized that something had happened to Lucius. Then I knew that Ringo had already seen it and that he knew what it was, so that when at last Louvinia came and told Granny, it was not as if Lucius had dared his mother to tell her but as if he had actually forced somebody, he didn't care who, to tell her. He had said it more than once, in the cabin one night probably for the first time, then after that in other places and to other people, to Negroes from other plantations even. Memphis was already gone then, and New Orleans, and all we had left of the River was Vicksburg and although we didn't believe it then, we wouldn't have that long. Then one morning Louvinia came in where Granny was cutting down the worn-out uniform pants Father had worn home from Virginia so they would fit me, and told Granny how Lucius was saying that soon the Yankees would have all of Mississippi and Yoknapatawpha county too, and all the niggers would be free, and that when that happened, he was going to be long gone. Lucius was working in the garden that morning. Granny went to the back gallery, still carrying the pants and the needle. She didn't even push her spectacles up. She said, "You, Lucius," just once, and Lucius came out of the garden with the hoe and Granny stood looking down at him over the spectacles as she looked over them at everything she did, from reading or sewing to watching the clock-face until the instant came to start burying the silver.
"You can go now," she said. "You needn't wait on the Yankees."
"Go?" Lucius said. "I ain't free."
"You've been free for almost three minutes," Granny said. "Go on."
Lucius blinked his eyes while you could have counted about ten. "Go where?" he said.
"I can't tell you," Granny said. "I ain't free. I would imagine you will have all Yankeedom to move around in."
Lucius blinked his eyes. He didn't look at Granny now. "Was that all you wanted?" he said.
"Yes," Granny said. So he went back to the garden. And that was the last we heard about being free from him.[122]

Faulkner also shows the Negro's childlike pleasure in small satisfactions:

He stood beside the car and watched Lucas cross the Square, toward the stores, erect beneath the old, fine, well-cared-for hat, walking with that unswerving and dignified deliberation which every now and then, and with something sharp at the heart, Edmonds recognized as having come from his own ancestry as the hat had come. He was not gone long. He returned, unhurried, and got into the car. He was carrying a small sack—obviously candy, a nickel's worth. He put it into Molly's hand.

"Here," he said. "You aint got no teeth left but you can gum it."[123]

Faulkner appreciates, too, the Negro's ability to serve with dignity:

After all, only a chosen few can accept service with dignity: it is man's impulse to do for himself. It rests with the servant to lend dignity to an unnatural proceeding.[124]

The personal experience Faulkner has had with Negroes and his respect for them are summed up in his dedication of *Go Down, Moses:*

> To Mammy
> Caroline Barr
> Mississippi
> 1840-1940

> Who was born in slavery and who gave to my family a fidelity without stint or calculation of recompense and to my childhood an immeasureable devotion and love[125]

Faulkner, through his Negroes, gives meaning to "courage and honor and hope and pride and compassion and pity and sacrifice."

Many of the same values are to be found in characterizations of the "poor white" tenant farmers. They are, however, more likely than the Negroes to be the victims of ambition. Of this the Snopeses are examples. Unable to bear the idea that there are some who have more than they the embittered tribe invades the entrenched domain of the county. Outside its bounds they would be small operators indeed, but here their trail is wide and noisome, and, unhappily, successful. This is not so much because the Snopeses themselves are especially clever as because those who might oppose them are unprepared for the attack when it comes. Before Varner is aware what has happened one Snopes has ousted him from his business. Bayard Sartoris fails to foresee what will come of his hiring another Snopes to work in the bank.

And yet, are the Snopeses really the victors? They may be, of course, in a material sense, but again readers may feel that Faulkner finds much more meaning in the peaceful wanderings of Ratliff, the remote quietness of the McCallums, and the persistent patience of the Bundrens. Whatever else the Snopeses may gain for themselves, they have attracted no willing converts. There is no evidence that even in a region like Beat Four there is any more selfish motive than old, misguided "honor" behind local activities. The Snopeses, Faulkner seems to be saying, have little chance of inheriting the earth while there are families like the Bundrens and the Armstids and the McCallums.

Faulkner admires these families for the fact that they have pride in themselves and in their small bits of land. Their wants are few and their generosity great. They have a philosophy which, while it may carry them no great distance in the material world, nevertheless serves

44

to give them courage to endure and to look upon their life with quiet satisfaction.

In the history of literature authors have occasionally appeared who could characterize the adolescent boy. Generally, however, these writers—Mark Twain with Tom Sawyer and Huck Finn, Booth Tarkington with the bashful lad of *Seventeen*—have exploited their young heroes for the humor that is in them. Faulkner's two memorable boys, Charley Mallison and Ike McCaslin, are different and in many ways more impressive. They are not only boys with all a boy's maddening qualities of indecision, self-assertion, and stubbornness. At the same time Faulkner shows us their incoherent gropings toward understanding, their yearning for maturity, their embarrassed awareness of beauty. Their emotions fly around like a weather vane in a hurricane. They are terrified and courageous; they are cautious and bold; they are childlike and adult; they are docile and mulish; they are disarming and infuriating. In other words, they are boys. Of the two Charley is the more convincing, since he is concerned with a genuine dilemma whereas we see Ike chiefly against the dreamlike background of the hunting camp. Ike is not burdened as Charley is with the problem of his mother:

. . . he remembered, it was two years ago now, he had finally made the high school football team or that is he had won or been chosen for one of the positions to make an out-of-town trip because the regular player had been injured in practice or fallen behind in his grades or maybe his mother wouldn't let him go, something, he had forgotten exactly what because he had been too busy all that Thursday and Friday racking his brains in vain to think how to tell his mother he was going to Mottstown to play on the regular team, right up to the last minute when he had to tell her something and so did; badly: and weathered it since his father happened to be present (though he really hadn't calculated it that way—not that he wouldn't have if he hadn't been too worried and perplexed with a blending of anger and shame and shame at being angry and ashamed ((crying at her at one point: 'Is it the team's fault that I'm the only child you've got?')) to think of it) and left that Friday afternoon with the team feeling as he imagined a soldier might feel wrenching out of his mother's restraining arms to go fight a battle for some shameful cause; she would grieve for him of course if he fell and she would even look on his face again if he didn't but there would always be ineradicable between them the ancient green and perennial adumbration: so that all Friday night trying to go to sleep in a strange bed and all the next forenoon waiting for the game to start he thought better for the team if he had not come since he had too much on his mind to be worth anything to it: until the first whistle blew and on and afterward until bottom-most beneath the piled mass of both teams, the ball clutched to his chest and his mouth and both nostrils full of the splashed dried whitewash marking the goal line he heard and recognized above all the others that one voice shrill triumphant and bloodthirsty and picked up at last and the wind thumped back into him he saw her foremost in the crowd not sitting in the grandstand but among the ones trotting and even running up and down the sideline following each play, then in the car that evening on the way back to Jefferson, himself in the front seat beside the hired driver and his mother and three of the other players in the back and her voice as proud and serene and pitiless as his own could have been: 'Does your arm still hurt?'[126]

Charley, on the other hand, is not called upon as Ike is to oppose his

45

courage to the great bear and to learn self-reliance the hardest way. Charley has Aleck Sander and Miss Habersham to accompany his grave-robbing. Ike is alone. There is more spiritual meaning in Ike's story, more practical meaning in Charley's. Whatever the meaning, however, Faulkner's touch upon the two characters is sure. We never know what they look like, but we are in no doubt as to what is in them of courage and honor and pity and pride.

Another of Faulkner's achievements in the field of characterization is that his animals are as real as his people. The dogs who hunt Old Ben are as important as the bear himself who evades them. His scorn of them is matched by their indiscreet courage in pursuing him. A little dog becomes real to us:

He had a little dog at home, a mongrel of the sort called a fyce by Negroes, a ratter, itself not much bigger than a rat and possessing that sort of bravery which had long since stopped being bravery and had become foolhardiness.[127]

Faulkner's mules, cross-grained and unpredictable, have personalities of their own:

They looked exactly like two ordinary, not extra good mules you might see in a hundred wagons on the road. I had done realized how they had a kind of jerky way of starting off, first one jerking into the collar and then jerking back and then the other jerking into the collar and then jerking back, and even after we was on the road and the wagon rolling good one of them taken a spell of some sort and snatched his self cross-ways in the traces like he aimed to turn around and go back, maybe crawling right across the wagon to do it, but then Stamper had told us they was a matched team; he never said they had ever worked together as a matched team, and they was a matched team in the sense that neither one of them seemed to have any idea as to just when the other one aimed to start moving.[128]

And it would be hard to find a more moving description than this one of old Bayard Sartoris's hound:

One of the dogs was quite old and nearly blind. It spent most of the day lying in the sun in the backyard or, during the hot summer day, in the cool dusty obscurity beneath the kitchen. But toward the middle of the afternoon it went around to the front and waited there quietly and gravely until the carriage came up the drive; and when Bayard had descended and entered the house it returned to the back and waited again until Isom led the mare up and Bayard came out and mounted. Then together they spent the afternoon going quietly and unhurriedly about the meadows and fields and woods in their seasonal mutations—the man on his horse and the ticked setter gravely beside him, while the descending evening of their lives drew toward its peaceful close upon the kind land that had bred them both.[129]

Each of Faulkner's animals has his own personality; each is memorable for himself; and not because of the human character to whom he is attached.

It is interesting to speculate about this particular ability of Faulkner's. Other novelists of the South, Ellen Glasgow and Marjorie Kinnan Rawlings, have the same skill at realizing the appeal in animals. The dog in *Vein of Iron*, a grave and stately setter, and the fawn in *The Yearling* are important characters and most attractive ones. One wonders whether these writers are successful because they themselves are fond of animals or whether they use them as characters with such effect because the people of whom they write are the sort who know and cherish animals as friends and respect them for their service. Whatever the reason, Faulkner handles his animal characters with the same perception he gives his people, and their actions do much to explain the human characters. Faulkner treats them with respect and with affection. They are seldom beautiful; their conduct is often ill-advised; they are frequently exasperating; but they are always real.

It would be omitting an important part of Faulkner's characterization to fail to mention his treatment of "things." As Wilson puts it, "For Faulkner everything man has made has the aspect of a human agent and the impact of a human meeting."[130] Thus the jail and the courthouse in Jefferson have personalities of their own.

But above all the courthouse: the center, the focus, the hub; sitting looming in the center of the county's circumference like a single cloud in its ring of horizon; musing, brooding, symbolic and ponderable, tall as cloud, solid as rock, dominating all; protector of the weak, judiciate and curb of the passions and lusts, repository and guardian of the aspirations and the hopes;[131]

This personification appears again and again: in Ratliff's elderly wagon, in Lucas Beauchamp's still, in barns and houses and tools and furnishings. It brings to many readers an added sense of "belonging" in the story and a heightened feeling of reality.

If one word could be used to sum up Faulkner's characters it might well be "alive." Each person, each animal, each object is distinct and vivid. Each has his own memorable qualities and each is a member of Faulkner's vast gallery of speaking likenesses.

FAULKNER'S CHRONOLOGY

As a result of Faulkner's method of presenting his characters bit by bit, readers are sometimes disturbed by what Beach has called his "riddling style, roundabout approach, lack of chronology, and confusing tricks to lead the reader astray and tease and bewilder him."[132] Certainly, however, an author is permitted by all the rules to present his story in the chronology which seems to him best and to withhold information until it can be given with the greatest impact. As Lubbock says in *The Craft of Fiction*, "The process of writing a novel is continual forestalling and anticipating. The author makes a point and reserves it; creates an effect and holds it back."[133] Faulkner's chronological methods, and his withholding of information seem justified, provided they are used to further his artistic purpose.

This it seems possible to prove if we recall what has been said about Faulkner's method of presenting his characters and if we realize that Faulkner's work cannot be fairly considered except as a whole. But most important to keep in mind is Faulkner's own stated purpose. He is showing us people in the light of their decisions between justice and injustice, courage and cowardice, pity and self.

As we have said, Faulkner presents his characters as they emerge in the particular situation he is describing, and at that moment of time. In Beach's words, Faulkner "establishes the front-stage drama well before showing us the back-stage motives."[134] He does not explain the past until it is needed to clarify a specific situation. Then at the proper moment, whenever that particular information can best be used, it is given. In *Intruder in the Dust,* for example, Charlie Mallison finds an unexpected confederate in Miss Habersham, one of the few remaining descendants of the original settlers of the county. He knows certain things about her, but one fact eludes him:

... only Miss Habersham remained: a kinless spinster of seventy living in the columned colonial house on the edge of town which had not been painted since her father died and had neither water nor electricity in it, with two Negro servants (and here again something nagged for an instant at his mind for attention but already in the same second gone, not even dismissed: just gone) in a cabin in the backyard, who (the wife) did the cooking while Miss Habersham and the man raised chickens and vegetables and peddled them about town from the pickup truck.[135]

None of this explains to Charlie why Miss Habersham should be so interested in the fate of Lucas Beauchamp. Then just when he must remember, he does:

... Miss Habersham called his name and his first impulse was to step quickly and quietly around the corner of the garage, from where he could reach the lot fence unseen and climb it and go on to the stable and so go out the pasture gate without passing the house again at all, flashlight or not but it was already too late; calling his name: 'Charles:' in that tense urgent whisper then came rapidly up and stopped facing him, speaking in that tense rapid murmur:
'What did he tell you?' and now he knew what it was that had nudged at his attention back in his uncle's office when he had recognized her and then in the next second flashed away: old Molly, Lucas' wife, who had been the daughter of one of old Doctor Habersham's, Miss Habersham's grandfather's, slaves, she and Miss Habersham the same age, born in the same week and both suckled at Molly's mother's breast and grown up together almost inextricably like sisters, like twins, sleeping in the same room, the white girl on the bed, the Negro girl on a cot at the foot of it almost until Molly and Lucas married, and Miss Habersham had stood up in the Negro church as godmother to Molly's first child.[136]

Sometimes the background material is so extensive that the story is dropped where it is, and we are returned to the earlier events and brought up to date again. Thus in *Light in August* we meet Joe Christmas when he arrives in town and starts working at the sawmill. We have no idea who he is or where he came from, but when we need that information we are returned to Joe's childhood, and given enough facts to account for his presence in Jefferson. As the story proceeds Hightower becomes an important figure. We must take time to learn about him. Finally Doc and Mrs. Hines appear in the town. As we find out who they are and why they have come we are able to fit more missing pieces into the picture of Joe. We had not realized they were missing; but we see finally how much they add to the richness of the portrait.

In *Absalom, Absalom* Faulkner by his chronological devices manages to add details just when they are most necessary. The story begins after all but one of the characters in it are dead—or are supposedly dead. The past is revealed as one incident recalls another, not as the events occurred in point of time. Thus the recollection of Sutpen's marriage leads to the memory of how he came to town as well as to the memory of how he died. The effect is one of doom, deepened by the fact that it is no secret at any time in the story that Sutpen met a violent end. The suspense is in the nature of the one small act which caused his death.

This is not to say that Faulkner cannot or will not tell a story "straight." Many of his short stories are developed along a clear narrative line, stories like "That Evening Sun" and "A Rose for Emily," "Pantaloon in Black" or "Go Down, Moses." *Intruder in the Dust* and *Sartoris* begin at the beginning and end at the end. But in the novels more than is possible in the short stories Faulkner makes use of digressions to convey the sense of the past.

It is obvious that Faulkner feels that this sense of the past is an important part of understanding people and the effect of their experiences upon them. For this reason he has chosen to limit himself as an author to a specific group of characters in a specific place, within a specific span of time. And it is an added reason for readers to consider his work as a whole. [If we read *Absalom, Absalom,* for example, we know almost all the story of the Sutpen family. But it is not until we have read "Wash" that we completely understand the most important incident. We may read *Requiem for a Nun* and understand it to our own satisfaction. But we will never know Temple Drake's story fully unless we have also read *Sanctuary,* nor will we altogether comprehend Nancy unless we have learned part of her story from "That Evening Sun."] We may learn in *The Hamlet* how the Snopes family came to the county, but we will never know who "the boy" is unless we have also read "Barn Burning." We may think we know all there is to know about Ike McCaslin when we have read "The Bear," but we are missing what we can learn about him in "Delta Autumn." And more than finding out about people by this method we gradually discover the long history of the county.

For some readers this mixture of the present and the past is tiresome and confusing. For others, however, it is one of the great attractions of Faulkner's work, since it gives a lifelike quality. Understanding it is as important as understanding the method Faulkner uses for presenting his characters to which we have referred. It is possible by this method for a reader to gain a very real sense of participating in the story of Yoknapatawpha county just as he may also participate in the life of his own town. If he is willing to wait, he will find unexpected facts adding to the fulness of his knowledge. In *Intruder in the Dust* Faulkner gives a brief glimpse of character in the course of a description of the jail:

... scratched into one of the panes of the fanlight beside the door was a young girl's single name, written by her own hand into the glass with a diamond in that same year (1864) and sometimes two or three times a year he would go up onto the gallery to look at it, it cryptic now in reverse, not for a sense of the past but to realise again the eternality, the deathlessness and changelessness of youth—the name of one of the daughters of the jailer of that time ... who stood at that window that afternoon and watched the battered remnant of a Confederate brigade retreat through the town, meeting suddenly across that space the eyes of the ragged unshaven lieutenant who led one of the broken companies, scratching into the glass not his name also, not only because a young girl of that time would never have done that but because she didn't know his name then, let alone that six months later he would be her husband.[137]

It is not until we read the section entitled "The Jail" in *Requiem for a Nun* that we find that the girl's name was Cecilia Farmer, that she was pale and frail and listless, that her father had taken the position as jailer because he had failed as a farmer, and that the young lieutenant came back to take her to his home in Alabama. What his name was we do not know.

Another effect of this method is that it serves Faulkner's need for creating suspense. Innuendo and hints are old tricks of the detective story writer, and legitimate devices in any novel. And in a very real sense Faulkner is presenting us with psychological detective stories. The question is seldom "Who did it?" but "Why did he do it?" Why did Henry Sutpen kill Charles Bon? Why did Charley Mallison feel that it was his moral responsibility to rescue Lucas? Why did Ab Snopes burn the Major de Spain's barn? The facts—the killing, the rescue, the barn burning—are well known to the reader. He also knows in each instance who did it. But it is Faulkner's aim to show him also why it was done, why it had to be done, and in the end what the doing meant to the doer.

This process, however, is not quite as simple as it sounds. Many readers find that at the end of one of Faulkner's books there is an unfinished effect. They have not learned all they want to know. The suspense has not quite been satisfied. This is another argument for considering Faulkner's work as a whole, since the answer those readers want may be in some other book already written or in one which will be written later.

Readers could not have expected in 1931 when *Sanctuary* and "That Evening Sun" were published that in twenty years' time those stories would be finished in *Requiem for a Nun*. When Quentin Compson committed suicide in 1929, so to speak, no one expected him to reemerge in 1936.

Few, in reading the earlier books, may have realized the need for any further information about the characters. Yet when it came in the later books many felt that the meaning of the first stories had been intensified and deepened and that suspense they had not known they felt had been satisfied. The only thing any reader may be sure of in Faulkner's work is that with over one hundred years of county history at his disposal, there is no knowing when we shall know everything there is to know about it, if indeed we ever shall.

FAULKNER'S STYLE

Like every artist except the dramatist, the novelist has only one medium through which to communicate his message. If his readers cannot understand him in his use of words he has said nothing. Therefore the writer's first task is to make himself comprehensible, and readers have every right to expect him to carry it out.

Quite properly fashions in writing have changed with changing times—have swung back and forth between the extremities of the wordiness of Scott and Cooper and the leanness of Crane and Hemingway. In general it may be safely said that the wordy style belongs to the romantic writer, and the lean one to the realist. Romantic writers have a tendency to want to tell the reader everything, and realists to feel that their job is to leave most of the decisions to their readers. This is a distinction most readers are ready for, and can recognize easily. But here again Faulkner is not quite what they expect as a stylist. Here again he is using the extra-realistic technique.

For Faulkner is not a romantic in his choice of material. He is dealing with what he considers real people with real problems and real decisions confronting them. But he is dealing with them from the inside. Therefore his writing must take on more than just a realistic tone. He cannot hope to make his people clear unless his readers know their innermost thoughts and look at the world through their eyes. We all know how disconnected our own thoughts are, how much comes into our minds by association, how many images occur to us which are beyond our words to express, but which we nevertheless feel deeply. We do not, for example, look at a small woolly cloud alone in a summer sky, and say to ourselves, "It looks just like a sheep." although that is what we may say aloud. We do not say much of anything to ourselves, but we feel the "sheepiness" of the cloud and extensions of meaning related perhaps to significant memory or idea. It is that feeling Faulkner tries to put into words. This is part of his concept of his artistic duty, because without knowing the depths of his people we cannot understand their surface actions. It imposes a strain on a reader who must learn to attribute to Faulkner's characters ideas and thoughts which he would never suspect them of having if he saw them only from the outside. It is what makes some of Faulkner's dialogue difficult—it contains not what such characters would actually say, but what their thoughts would say. It is also what makes some of his description difficult—

51

it is not the description of what a reader thinks the character would or should see, but of what the character does see.

The technique is difficult, because it is not common, and Faulkner does not always bring it off successfully. More often, though, a reader may not be reading with care, sometimes because he has been too recently involved in a passage which seemed perfectly matter-of-fact. Another answer to apparent weaknesses is that Faulkner's style is in a perpetual state of change and development, with consequent variation from book to book, from story to story. But if his purpose is understood, and if a reader is willing to give himself up to this element in Faulkner's work, the problem of his style becomes far less overwhelming. And eventually the result Faulkner is striving for is the one achieved. Readers feel what they are expected to feel: complete identity with the characters.

Actually, this is probably making the question of Faulkner's style too formidable. Many critics have done that in the past, and many readers have been frightened by it. Faulkner has been made to sound like a genius in the art of obscurity. Much criticism of Faulkner's style has emphasized only the hazards in his fiction: that the prose style seems to be a test Faulkner has set for himself to unravel;[138] that it is "oblique, involuted, circumambient";[139] that the author often gets involved in endless sentences trying to wring everything out of what he says;[140] that Faulkner's rhetoric is (to quote Yeats) "will doing the work of the imagination";[141] that his rhetoric is "the most elaborate, intermittently incoherent, and ungrammatical, thunderous, polyphonic in American literature."[142] And who would not be discouraged by a newspaper review that started:

Because William Faulkner is the most recent winner of the Nobel Prize in Literature, it is obvious he is one of the world's great novelists. But there are thousands of persons who have been unable to finish his books because he insists on writing such long sentences and bringing in material that has to be fitted into place after much thought. His new novel contains some of his sharpest writing and most provocative thinking and some of his most exasperating prose. When you learn that one sentence here is 49 pages long you will get a general idea.[143]

What price the "sharpest writing" and the "most provocative thinking" in the face of that forty-nine page sentence? The reader of the review is not told that the famous sentence consists of a series of independent clauses carefully punctuated with semicolons, and that each clause could be diagrammed by a patient high school student. It is unlikely that many readers will be encouraged to buy or read the book to find its quality for themselves.

In a recent book, *The Poetics of Music*, the composer Igor Stravinsky quotes Baudelaire on the subject of the artistic discipline Faulkner has been accused of flouting:

It is evident that rhetorics and prosodies are not abritrarily invented tyrannies, but a collection of rules demanded by the very organization of the spiritual being.

and never have prosodies and rhetorics kept originality from fully manifesting itself. The contrary, that is to say that they have aided the flowering of originality, would be infinitely more true.[144]

It takes only a little study to discover that Faulkner knows and respects the rules of rhetoric as well as any author. His originality is clearly developed within them. His sentences, long though some of them are, have the necessary ingredients, and his frequent use of parentheses should make no trouble for readers who know for what reasons parentheses appear. Naturally, long sentences are surprising after a long dearth of involved writing, and probably any readers whose standards have been set by Rudolph Flesch feel resentful toward elaborate effects; but there is no reason to feel that Faulkner's sentences are incomprehensible merely because of their length. Faulkner does not, it must be clearly understood, keep his readers in a perpetual marathon to get to the end of the sentence; and too much insistence upon this point may be misleading. He can be admirably succinct when that type of sentence is required.

Luster gave her the hat and he and Ben went on across the backyard. Ben was still whimpering, though not loud. Dilsey and Frony went to the cabin. After a while Dilsey emerged, again in the faded calico dress, and went to the kitchen. The fire had died down. There was no sound in the house. She put on the apron and went up stairs. There was no sound anywhere. Quentin's room was as they had left it. She entered and picked up the undergarment and put the stocking back in the drawer and closed it. Mrs. Compson's door was closed. Dilsey stood beside it for a moment, listening. Then she opened it and entered, entered a pervading reek of camphor. The shades were drawn, the room in halflight, and the bed, so that at first she thought Mrs. Compson was asleep and was about to close the door when the other spoke.[145]

And always in the long sentences where punctuation is needed it is used with respect for all its possibilities of deepening the meaning:

Because they were too busy raging and sweating among the dismantled logs and felling the new ones in the adjacent woods and trimming and notching and dragging them out and mixing the tenuous clay mud to chink them together with; it was not until the second day that they learned what was troubling Ratcliffe, because now they had time, the work going no slower, no lessening of sweat but on the contrary, if anything the work going even a little faster because now there was a lightness in the speed and all that was abated was the rage and the outrage, because somewhere between the dark and the dawn of the first and second day, something had happened to them—the men who had spent that first long hot endless July day sweating and raging about the wrecked jail, flinging indiscriminately and savagely aside the dismantled logs and the log-like laudanum-smitten inmates in order to rebuild the one, cursing old Holston and the lock and the four—three—bandits and the eleven militia-men who had arrested them, and Compson and Pettigrew and Peabody and the United States of America—the same men met at the project before sunrise on the next day which was already promising to be hot and endless too, but with the rage and the fury absent now, quiet, not grave so much as sobered, a little amazed, diffident, blinking a little perhaps, looking a little aside from one another, a little unfamiliar even to one another in the new jonquil-colored light, looking about them at the meagre huddle of crude cabins set without order and every one a little awry to every other and all dwarfed to dollhouses by the vast loom of the woods which enclosed them—the tiny clearing clawed punily not even into the flank of pathless wilderness, but into the loin, the groin, the secret parts, which was the irrevocable cast die of their lives, fates, pasts and futures—not even speaking for a while yet since each one probably believed (a little shamefaced too) that the thought was solitarily his, until at last one spoke for all and then it was all right since it had taken one conjoined breath to shape that sound, the speaker speaking not loud, diffidently, tentatively, as you insert the first light tentative push of wind into the mouthpiece of a strange untried foxhorn: 'By God. Jefferson.'[146]

In fact, to readers interested in punctuation as a technical device Faulkner's work is a gold mine. In many ways his use of it is reminiscent of Laurence Sterne's. Dashes are frequent, quotation marks and apostrophes are frequently omitted, and commas are sparingly used in the places where we are accustomed to find them. A comma as Faulkner uses it means something important and had better not be overlooked. Colons appear often, and always for a well-defined reason. A long dialogue in "The Bear"[147] between Ike McCaslin and his cousin is an ample illustration of Faulkner's brilliant and meaningful use of what most readers have come to regard automatically. Here the only words used to indicate the speakers are "and he" (Ike) and "and McCaslin" (the cousin). These are placed at the end of the previous speaker's words instead of at the beginning of the character's own speech—a device which gives the needed effect of one speaker rushing in upon the other:

. . . and he

'I am free:' and this time McCaslin did not even gesture, no inference of fading pages, no postulation of the stereoptic whole, but the frail and iron thread strong as truth and impervious as evil and longer than life itself and reaching beyond record and patrimony both to join him with the lusts and passions, the hopes and dreams and griefs, of bones whose names while still fleshed and capable even old Carothers' grandfather had never heard: and he:

'And of that too:' and McCaslin

'Chosen, I suppose (and I will concede it) out of all your time by Him, as you say Buck and Buddy were from theirs. And it took Him a bear and an old man and four years just for you. And it took you fourteen years to reach that point and about that many, maybe more, for Old Ben, and more than seventy for Sam Fathers. And you are just one. How long then? How long.' and he

'It will be long. I have never said otherwise. But it will be all right because they will endure —' and McCaslin

'And anyway, you will be free. — No, not now nor ever, we from them and they from us. So I repudiate too. I would deny even if I knew it were true. I would have to. Even you can see that I could do no else. I am what I am; I will be always what I was born and have always been. And more than me. More than me, just as there were more than Buck and Buddy in what you called His first plan which failed:' and he

'And more than me:' and McCaslin

'No, Not even you. Because mark. You said how on that instant when Ikkemotubbe realized that he could sell the land to Grandfather, it ceased forever to have been his. All right; go on: Then it belonged to Sam Fathers, old Ikkemotubbe's son. And who inherited from Sam Fathers, if not you. Co-heir perhaps with Boon, if not of his life maybe, at least of his quitting it?' and he

'Yes. Sam Fathers set me free.'[148]

In the midst of this dialogue is a twenty page speech by Ike,[149] during which he quotes several earlier conversations, using the conventional introductory words. The unwary reader of these twenty pages, seeing the words "said McCaslin" instead of "and McCaslin" is likely to think he is back in the original dialogue and consequently to become hopelessly confused about what is going on. When he suddenly returns to "and he" and "and McCaslin" on page 315, he may do one of two things. He may go back and reread the passage, or he may dismiss the whole thing with the thought that Faulkner is just careless about his work, and that none of it makes sense anyway—which it certainly does not by that method of reading. Difficulties like these probably were at the root of Malcolm Cowley's remark that Faulkner rewards and deserves a second reading.[150]

Distinct from critical condemnation of Faulkner's rhetoric has been equal condemnation of his use of words as words. While Breit uses the more kindly interpretation, "spectacular,"[151] Beach is uncompromising with his "extravagant."[152] Both Beach and Wilson see an Elizabethan quality in his writing.[153] Beach, however, says that it lapses into Jacobean—"strength and passion haunting a charnel house."[154] As for Faulkner's use of figurative language, Linn and Taylor find him dissolving actuality in a welter of images—"products of his morbid imagination."[155] Campbell considers Faulkner's metaphors faulty because of the impression of effort they give, their lack of logic, and the use of words whose effect is not metaphorical.[156] Beach calls them "nonchalant."[157]

Although many readers have been appalled by the length of Faulkner's sentences, as we have noted, it is more probable that the actual difficulty has come not from the length but from what might well be called the "welter." Certainly it sometimes seems like nothing more:

Because that's what a Southern lady is. Not the fact that, penniless and with no prospect of ever being otherwise and knowing that all who know her know this, yet moving with a parasol and a private chamber pot and three trunks into your home and into the room where your wife uses the hand-embroidered linen, she not only takes command of all the servants who likewise know that she will never tip them, because they know as well as the white folks that she will never have anything to tip them with, but goes into the kitchen and dispossesses the cook and seasons the very food you are going to eat to suit her own palate—it's not this, not this that she is depending on to keep body and soul together: it is as though she were living on the actual blood itself, like a vampire, not with insatiability, certainly not with voracity, but with that serene and idle splendor of flowers abrogating to herself, because it fills her veins also, nourishment from the old blood that crossed uncharted seas and continents and battled wilderness hardships and lurking circumstances and fatalities.[158]

There do seem to be a great many more words than are necessary, often more images than many readers find comfortable, some which may even be hard to understand. The meaning of a sentence may be hard to find in its lush surroundings. And in some instances readers may feel that the meaning, when it is found, is too slight to need such embellishment.

It was not even an ultimatum, it was a simple instruction, a decree, impersonal, the mail rider now well into the fringe of the group, saying nothing and missing nothing, like a weightless dessicated or fossil bird, not a vulture of course nor even quite a hawk, but say a pterodactyl chick arrested just out of the egg ten glaciers ago and so old in simple infancy as to be the worn and weary ancestor of all subsequent life.[159]

There is no gainsaying that this verbal richness has been one of the greatest difficulties for Faulkner's readers, nor can it be denied that it has a difficult quality. It may be possible to discover, however, that it need not be as great a problem as it has been made to seem, and that with care it may be found to be one of the assets of Faulkner's work.

The first thing to note is an inescapable fact of modern life. Books are coming off the presses at a much greater rate than ever before. It is the duty of the critic to read and evaluate them. It is a reader's pleasure (sometimes regarded as a social obligation) to read them. If he does not wish to buy he may borrow. The latter process costs less money, but is accompanied by the uneasy feeling that another reader is waiting eagerly for him to finish. Leisurely reading is not expected in the modern scene. Critics can hardly afford it, nor can readers. Leisurely reading, however, is what Faulkner requires. He is presenting a large and varied group of characters against a rich and colorful background, and he is trying to make every figure and every moment vivid, real, and memorable. But the whole effect cannot be grasped in a hurry by even the most skilled readers.

If, however, time is taken—plenty of time—much of difficulty disappears. There is opportunity to notice the heaping up of figures to achieve full understanding, to read long, involved sentences twice or three times if need be, to untangle the seeming mazes of dashes, parentheses, parentheses within parentheses, to notice what Faulkner has accomplished with his words. Whether a reader is satisfied with Faulkner's accomplishment depends upon whether that reader feels convinced of Faulkner's purpose. His decision should not be conditioned by hasty judgment of what may at first seem to be verbal confusion.

It seems safe to assume that Faulkner is a serious writer, not interested in playing with or tricking his readers with displays of his erudite vocabulary. He is primarily desirous of giving a reader the fullest possible understanding of his characters as they make their choices between justice and injustice, courage and cowardice, sacrifice and greed, pity and self. For this reason he seems to feel that it is necessary to leave nothing to chance or to misunderstanding. He wants to make his readers comprehend not only with their minds but with their imaginations and with all their senses. Where a quality may not be clear to the eyes it may be vividly heard or smelled or felt, and at the same time realized through intelligence and memory:

. . . then he was in the chair again in front of the new bright and swirling fire, enveloped in the quilt like a cocoon, enclosed completely now in the unmistakable odor of Negroes—that smell which if it were not for something that was going to happen to him within a space of minutes he would have gone to his grave never once pondering speculating if perhaps that smell were really not the odor of a race nor even actually of poverty but perhaps of a condition: an idea: a belief: an acceptance, a passive acceptance by them themselves of the idea that being Negroes they were not supposed to have facilities to wash properly or often or even to wash bathe often even without the facilities to do it with; that in fact it was a little to be preferred that they did not.[160]

And if a quality may be understood through all the senses, Faulkner gives us each sensation:

Tennie's Jim waked him at three. He dressed rapidly, shivering, not so much from the cold because a fresh fire already boomed and roared on the hearth, but in that dead winter hour when the blood and the heart are slow and sleep is incomplete. He crossed the gap between house and kitchen, the gap of iron earth beneath the brilliant and rigid night where the dawn would not begin for three hours yet, tasting, tongue, palate, and to the very bottom of his lungs, the searing dark, and entered the kitchen, the lamp-lit warmth where the stove glowed, fogging the windows, and where Boon already sat at the table at breakfast, his working jaws blue with stubble, and his face innocent of water and his coarse, horse-man hair innocent of comb.[161]

This descriptive method may make some readers impatient, but to others it is an enriched experience.

Another aspect of this characteristic of Faulkner's writing is that as an author he believes in his artistic purpose. He is involved not only intellectually but emotionally in his work. This is abundantly clear in his attitude toward his characters as well as toward their situations. He could not write of them with such care and interest if he did not himself feel love and pity for them. This being so, it seems probable that Faulkner, like many other writers, expresses his own emotional concern through the elaboration of his style.

Of course it may be argued that Faulkner carries his emotional involvement too far, that he reaches the point of being "drunk with the sound of his own words." This is something a reader must decide for himself, but he should at least decide on the basis of his own reading experience in Faulkner's work, and not on the word of a critic who may be impatient because, as he reads, he is short of time.

The sight of many pages in any book of Faulkner's without a sign of a paragraph, with no indication of dialogue, with a minimum of punctuation, and with no proper names may lead readers to wonder just what the method of presentation is. Does Faulkner ask his readers merely to read about what has already happened or are they to be given the opportunity to see events happen for themselves? Readers of fiction generally expect to see the characters in action and to be allowed to judge the meaning of the action.

The whole subject of presentation of material is admirably discussed by Percy Lubbock in *The Craft of Fiction*. Lubbock defines two methods: the pictorial, in which action is seen through the emotions of the character, and in which a reader is not really looking *at* the events as they occur, but is hearing *about* them; and the dramatic, in which the mood of the character is of less importance than the action.[162] In a scene presented pictorially a reader faces the author and listens to him, while the author in turn has his attention fixed on the form and color of the incident in the thought of the character.[163] In a scene presented dramatically the reader faces the story and watches it, while the author has his attention on the action involved in the incident itself.[164] Most authors use both methods, but Lubbock suggests that examples of generally pictorial writers would be Fielding, Balzac, and Scott, while Tolstoy, Dostoievski, and DeMaupassant are generally dramatic.[165]

Lubbock goes on to cite the disadvantages of each method. The pictorial presentation, he says, may drag in the author too obviously, and may make for general thinness of impression. There is an air of ineffectiveness and the story loses in intensity if the characters are standing still while the author talks about them. On the other hand, the dramatic method is too limited when the action must not only be placed in view but must be related to its surroundings. Action alone gives only limited vision and a scene recreated by a character's memory cannot express outlying association.[166] Sometimes, also, dramatic presentation may be too strong. It may make the action seem harsh, overcharged or romantic.[167] At such times it may be more real by the use of the narrator. At other times incidents may not accommodate themselves to the reader's point of view without the aid of the narrator to look at the facts and create an impression of them for him.[168] One further limitation of the dramatic method is that it shows action essentially and does not give an inner picture of the character's mind.

Like most authors Faulkner uses both methods to present his material, but in many instances a scene which another writer might treat dramatically is handled by Faulkner as a pictorial incident. The fact that many of his short stories and many of the scenes in his novels are dramatic indicates that he is certainly aware of this type of presentation and leads to the question: why does he so often use the pictorial method? With Lubbock's words in mind it may be helpful to consider possible reasons.

We know that Faulkner believes that all of the past of the county and of its people helps to condition the actions of the present. Therefore each event is the result of some earlier happening, and a reader may fail to understand its significance fully unless he is aware at the same time of what went before. Often, as Faulkner presents his material out of chronological order, that past event has never been mentioned until the present one (of which it is the cause) is about to take place. This past event may be presented to the reader by Faulkner as narrator because the character is unaware of it (as in the story of Miss Burden in *Light in August*). Joe Christmas has met her, but he has no interest in her past. Readers do have an interest, however, because unless they know who she is and where she came from they will be unable to understand her presence in Jefferson. Therefore Faulkner stops the narrative of the present to supply this information. In another incident a reader may not be aware of any need to understand the past, but it will come by association into the mind of the character involved. This is what happens when Ratliff sees Ab Snopes and is reminded of the time he and Ab went to town to get the separator and became involved in a horse trade. Now the reader pauses as Ratliff recollects, and the result is a story within a story. Of course, detailed scenes are presented dramatically, but the overall impression is of the relationships between such incidents.

Another reason Faulkner presents some scenes pictorially when they might be susceptible of dramatic treatment is perhaps that he thinks they might be, in Lubbock's words, "harsh, overcharged, or romantic." Thus we do not see either Miss Burden or Rider die. These scenes are lurid enough as they are described without the necessity of witnessing them. We never know what was said when Anse Bundren proposed to his new bride, and we really know only the outside edges of the story of "A Rose for Emily." Our imaginations work overtime, but it is we who make the picture, through suggestion, not creation, by Faulkner.

Since much of Faulkner's fiction concerns itself with what is going on in the minds of his characters, as well as with what is happening to them, a great deal of his writing describes their thoughts and reactions to outside events. This description, of course, is needful for a reader if he is to understand the character as fully as Faulkner feels he must. The result of it is that many pages are devoted not to action at all but to a character's attempts to evaluate and understand previous action. Sometimes the character's thoughts are presented in the "stream of consciousness" manner, representing what is passing through his mind at a given moment, just as it occurs, and whether or not it is relevant to the matter in hand.

But there was until the three quarters anyway, except *suppose seeing on the rushing darkness only his own face no broken feather unless the two of them but not two like that going to Boston the same night then my face his face for an instant across the crashing when out of darkness two lighted windows in rigid fleeing crash gone his face and mine just I see saw did I see not goodbye the marquee empty of eating the road empty in darkness in silence the bridge arching into silence darkness sleep the water peaceful and swift not goodbye.*[169]

Sometimes only his thoughts which directly concern the immediate question are recorded.

It's because she wants it told, he thought, so that people whom she will never see and whose names she will never hear and who have never heard her name nor seen her face will read it and know at last why God let us lose the War: that only through the blood of our men and the tears of our women could He stay this demon and efface his name and lineage from the earth.[170]

Often Faulkner uses the character's memory to supply background for present incidents.

But he had already thought of that too, remembering his grandfather telling of the old days when deer and bear and wild turkey could be hunted in Yoknapatawpha County within twelve miles of Jefferson, of the hunters: Major de Spain who had been his grandfather's cousin and old General Compson and Uncle Ike McCaslin, Carothers Edmonds' great-uncle, still alive at ninety, and Boon Hoggenbeck whose mother had been a Chickasaw woman and Negro Sam Fathers whose father had been a Chickasaw chief, and Major de Spain's one-eyed hunting mule Alice who wasn't afraid even of the smell of bear and he thought how if you really were the sum of your ancestry it was too bad the ancestors who had evoluted him into a secret ressurector of country graveyards hadn't thought to equip him with a descendant of that unspookable one-eyed mule to transport his subjects on.[171]

Some readers occasionally find difficulties in Faulkner's presentation of this material, because the change from fact, from the narrative that Faulkner himself is telling, to the thoughts of the character is not clearly indicated. Faulkner generally shows the change by placing the thought material in italics or by omitting punctuation altogether or by using the introductory words "he thought." It is possible, however, for a reader who is reading too fast to overlook these signs. And sometimes what the character is thinking goes on for such a long time and contains so much dialogue and narrative that a reader may forget that he is not reading the same story he began and is not ready for the return to it when it actually comes. Faulkner uses a few chapter divisions, and one chapter may contain both direct and indirect narration. This is especially true in *Absalom, Absalom!*, and this makes it one of Faulkner's most confusing pieces of work. If, however, a reader is alert to the possiblity of these shifts he may find that through them Faulkner is enabled to give a much deeper and rounder picture of his characters than he would be able to give if he depended more upon showing people in action and less upon showing the effect upon them of that action.

But Faulkner's novels are by no means monsters of descriptive writing. It is true that his characters remember a great deal and remember it more coherently than readers might expect, and they spend a great deal of time pondering the meaning of what has happened or what seems about to happen. But they also talk. While their conversation is often cryptic because it concerns matters which readers may have overlooked or matters which are clear to the characters but will only be explained to a reader by subsequent events, this obscurity does not need to be the obstacle some readers have made it. The answer exists and will be discovered at its proper place in the narrative.

Whatever use Faulkner makes of dialogue, and no matter how difficult it may be to interpret in terms of relationship to character or incident, most readers find that it is brilliantly accurate in diction. Faulkner's Negroes sound like Negroes:

"One day we wuz gwine along a road. It wuz a busted-up road and it didn't look like no M.P. country. But day wuz some of 'em in de las' town we dodged, so we didn't know we wuz so close to whar de war wuz gwine on 'twell we walked on to a bridge and come right on a whole regiment of Germans swimmin' in de river. Dey seed us about de same time we seed dem and div under de water, and me and de other boy grabbed up two machine guns settin' dar and we sot on de bridge rail, and ev'y time a German stuck his haid up fer a new breaf, us shot 'im. It was jes' like shootin' turkles in a slough. I reckon dey wuz close to a hund'ed us kilt 'fo' de machine guns run dry. Dat's whut dey gimme dis fer." He drew from his pocket a florid, plated medal of Porto Rican origin, and Isom came quietly up to see.

"Umuhuh," Simon said. He sat with his hands on his knees watching his son with rapt astonishment. Elnora came up also, her hands daubed with flour.

"Whut does dey look like?" she asked. "Like folks?"

"Dey's big," Caspey answered. "Sort of pink lookin' and about eight feet tall. Only folks in de whole American war dat could handle 'um wuz de cullud regiments."[172]

And Faulkner's poor whites speak with authentic accent:

"How'd you like the army, Buddy?" Bayard asked.

"Not much," Buddy answered. "Ain't enough to do. Good life for a lazy man." He mused a moment. "They gimme a charm," he added in a burst of shy diffident confidence and sober pleasure.

"A charm?" Bayard repeated.

"Uhuh. One of them brass gimcracks on to a colored ribbon. I aimed to show it to you, but I fergot. Do it tomorrow. That 'ere flo's too cold to tech till I have to. I'll watch a chance tomomrrow when pappy's outen the house."

"Why? Don't he know you got it?"

"He knows," Buddy answered. "Only he don't like it because he claims it's a Yankee charm. Rafe says pappy and Stonewall Jackson ain't never surrendered."[173]

For many readers, one of the greatest pleasures in Faulkner's writing is to be found in such passages as these. It lies not only in the accuracy of the diction, but just as much in Faulkner's telling descriptions of the speakers.

Faulkner is using dialogue, however, not merely to give a picture of the character as he seems at the surface. It is not, therefore, strictly the dialogue of dramatic presentation. In Faulkner's work, just as the character's thoughts are clues to what he will do if confronted with a choice between justice and injustice, courage and cowardice, sacrifice and greed, pity and self, so every word he utters is another clue. Faulkner's dialogues are often exact expressions of thought, and they can be understood only if we are conscious of what those thoughts probably are. The words spoken are a kind of shorthand, and the characters whose minds are thus communicating know what they mean. Many readers find this interpretive problem difficult and would rather have everything stated explicitly, but for others it is one of the most challenging reading experiences in modern fiction.

The total effect of Faulkner's style in narrative, description, and dialogue is one of extraordinary richness, of "exuberant and tropical luxuriance."[174] According to Aiken, "Small wonder if even the most passionate of Mr. Faulkner's admirers ... must find, with each new novel that the first fifty pages are always the hardest, that each time one must learn all over again how to read this strangely fluid and slippery and heavily mannered prose, and that one is even . . . sometimes tempted to give it up."[175] As Aiken goes on to say, however, once a reader is thoroughly immersed in Faulkner's writing, he wants to remain that way.[176] It seems possible to deduce two reasons for this. One is that much of Faulkner's writing gives the effect of poetry and much of it is beautiful. Reading many of his descriptive passages may give a purely sensuous pleasure. The other is that the style is a clue to the meaning of the novels themselves. In its involution and suspension of climax and adding of detail to detail until the final revelation it is significant of the same qualities in Faulkner's plots and characterizations. It is difficult to see how he could make his stories the powerful emotional experiences they are to many readers without the style he has developed.

CONCLUSION

In dealing with the work of an author whose achievement is the subject of controversy it is well to keep in mind the words of F. L. Lucas in his introduction to his edition of the plays of John Webster:

An attempt to answer them (indictments) fairly is after all more likely to reveal the dramatist's real qualities than a great deal of beating the air with vague gestures of panegyric. It is too easy to pile mere flowers of speech on a grave like Webster's; in a day or two it is the flowers that are dead. The essential is not to praise but to try to understand.[177]

The verdict on any author is of doubtful value unless it is backed by a sincere effort to understand him and what he is trying to do. Thus far I have tried to collect evidences as to Faulkner's ethical and artistic ideas, his style and his method in order to contribute to that understanding. It would, therefore, be unfair to attempt to deny that his writing is often difficult, and that his style in his latest books is more involved than in his early work; that he is guilty of occasional lapses of grammar and that he sometimes appears to be too much in love with a specific word; that his choice of words is generally for the Latinism; and that occasionally he loses track of his characters. But is Faulkner's occasional carelessness serious enough to affect the importance of his total achievement?

It is the total achievement which now becomes the point to determine. Is it great enough to place him among the important figures in American fiction, or does it merely insure him a place among the also-rans, vaguely noted in ten years, forgotten in fifty? Are we to believe Warren when he says, "The study of Faulkner is the most challenging single task in contemporary American literature for criticism to undertake,"[178] or are we to side with Geismar's statement that "Faulkner's is the history of dissipated talent"?[179]

If we summarize our discoveries about Faulkner we must admit that

62

he is writing from moral conviction and that he has a thesis to prove in his novels; that he is presenting that thesis through a group of characters related to each other in time, place, and heritage; that his characters, his setting, and his situations are in sufficient variety and yet sufficiently unified to give a broad and at the same time consistent view of human experience; and that the effect upon readers may well be a heightened response and understanding both of themselves and of life. We have also discovered that although his style may present initial difficulties, his technical innovations can be justified by the effects he gains through them. In other words we have discovered that a reader is justified in considering Faulkner a serious if controversial novelist.

A serious and controversial novelist has a place in any literature. A serious and controversial novelist will always find readers. A reader of taste, Miss Drew says, has a "gusto for life, and curiosity to meet as much of it as possible."[180] He is a "good hater," but is not the victim of prejudice, and in his reading he will make "likes and dislikes account for themselves,"[181] provided he believes that the author means what he says. A reader of taste has no interest in fighting a straw man. He is anxious to meet the challenge of a serious one. The discovery and appreciation of a new talent is always alluring to such a reader and he is interested in the possiblity of a reading experience like Andre Gide's:

I have to admit that it took me some time to become acclimated to the latter (Faulkner), although I now regard him as one of the most important, perhaps *the* most important, of the stars in this new constellation.[182]

To the same point Howard Mumford Jones quotes Mr. Ken McCormick, editor-in-chief of Doubleday and Company:

The idea that subtlety, insight and artistic distinction in writing can be only for the intelligent chosen few is tiresome intellectual snobbery. That the ability to communicate to large numbers of readers automatically means undistinguished writing and indiscrimate detail and subject matter is equally specious.[183]

The latter clause of this statement is interesting in view of the fact that many of Faulkner's best short stories, in both structure and ethics have been published in one of the most widely read American weekly magazines.

If we concede Faulkner the right to make a place for himself in American literature we ought to speculate on what that place might be in relation to other authors. It is not the purpose of this paper to make a comparative study of Faulkner's writing, but it is worth noting that critics who have done so have found a bewildering array of relationships. Cowley finds, for example, that in Faulkner's early work there is mention or echo of Keats, Balzac, Flaubert, Swinburne, Mallarme, Wilde, Housman, Joyce, Eliot, Sherwood Anderson, E. E. Cummings, and Scott Fitzgerald.[184] Hartwick also sees the resemblance to Swinburne in what he calls Faulkner's "clever and dappled" language.[185] On another page, however, the same author places Faulkner in the tradition of Stephen Crane.[186] Geismar stems Faulkner's technical virtuosity from the French Symbolists, and from Proust, Yeats, Joyce, Freud and Einstein.[187] He also sees him influenced by Bearsley, Wilde, Huxley, Mencken, and the Elizabethans. His contemporaries include Allen Tate, Wolfe, Paul Green, and Caldwell.[188] Snell traces Faulkner's "apocalyptical vision" to Charles Brockden Brown;[189] Beach sees Faulkner's subject matter resembling Poe's, his chronology like Conrad's, and his psychological mystery like both Conrad and James.[190] To Conrad, Wilson adds Joyce and Proust;[191] and Breit agrees to Joyce but makes the new addition of Donne.[192] Starke sees the short stories as demonstrating Faulkner's intention to produce a comedy in the tradition of Balzac, Cabell, Galsworthy and Van Vechten.[193]

From this collection one fact should emerge clearly: Faulkner is Faulkner. But such comparisons are also an indication that his appeal is not limited to one type of reader. It is probable that no one reader will like all of Faulkner's work, but it is equally probable that almost any reader will like some of it. Those who enjoy tightly plotted work will find reading pleasure in many of the short stories; those who like subjective writing will find it in both novels and short stories. Faulkner's work has plenty of humor, plenty of action, plenty of local color, plenty of mood. And there is, finally, plenty of purpose in the writing. Whether Faulkner is greater in his short stories or in his novels is a question that a reader must decide for himself, or leave unanswered as he wishes. But no matter what a reader selects of Faulkner's work he will find in it the clear statement that the important values in life are qualities like "courage and honor and hope and pride and compassion and pity and sacrifice," and that they are achieved only through the constant choice between justice and injustice, courage and cowardice, sacrifice and greed, pity and self.

It would seem that as an artist Faulkner has in mind the words with which Conrad memorably described the duty of the writer:

My task which I am trying to achieve is, by the power of the written word to make you hear, to make you feel—it is, before all, to make you *see*. That—and no more, and it is everything. If I succeed, you shall find there according to your deserts: encouragement, consolation, fear, charm—all you demand—and perhaps, also that glimpse of truth for which you have forgotten to ask.[194]

BIBLIOGRAPHY

Books by William Faulkner

Absalom, Absalom!, New York, Modern Library, 1951
As I Lay Dying, New York, Modern Library, 1946
Collected Stories, New York, Random House, 1950
Go Down, Moses, New York, Random House, 1942
The Hamlet, New York, Random House, 1940
Intruder in the Dust, New York, Random House, 1948
Knight's Gambit, New York, Random House, 1949
Light in August, New York, Modern Library, 1950
Mosquitoes, New York, Boni and Liveright, 1927
The Portable Faulkner, Malcolm Cowley, ed., New York, Viking Press, 1951
Requiem for a Nun, New York, Random House, 1951
Sanctuary, New York, Modern Library, 1931
Sartoris, New York, Harcourt Brace, 1951
Soldiers' Pay, New York, Liveright, 1926
The Sound and the Fury, New York, Modern Library, 1946
The Wild Palms, New York, Random House (Penguin Books), 1948

Books about the Novel and about Faulkner

Aiken, Conrad, "William Faulkner: The Novel as Form," in Frederick J. Hoffman
and Olga W. Vickery, eds., *William Faulkner, Two Decades of Criticism,* (East
Lansing, Michigan State College Press, 1951)
Beach, Joseph Warren, *American Fiction 1920-1940,* New York, Macmillan, 1941
Breit, Harvey, Introduction to *Absalom, Absalom!* by William Faulkner, New York,
Modern Library, 1951
Conrad, Joseph, *The Nigger of the "Narcissus,"* New York, Doubleday, 1947
Cowley, Malcolm, Introduction to *The Portable Faulkner,* New York, Viking Press,
1951
De Voto, Bernard, *The World of Fiction,* Boston, Houghton Mifflin, 1950
Drew, Elizabeth A., *The Modern Novel,* New York, Harcourt Brace, 1926
Geismar, Maxwell, "A Cycle of Fiction," in Spiller's *Literary History of the United
States,* New York, Macmillan, 1948
Geismar, Maxwell, *Writers in Crisis,* Boston, Houghton Mifflin, 1942
Gide, Andre, *Imaginary Interviews,* translated by Malcolm Cowley, New York,
Knopf, 1944
Hartwick, Harry, *The Foreground of American Fiction,* New York, American Book
Company, 1934
James, Henry, *The Art of Fiction and Other Essays,* New York, Oxford, 1948
Kazin, Alfred, *On Native Grounds,* New York, Reynal and Hitchcock, 1942
Linn, James Weber, and Taylor, Houghton Wells, *A Forward to Fiction,* New York,
D. Appleton-Century, 1935
Lubbock, Percy, *The Craft of Fiction,* New York, Jonathan Cape and Harrison
Smith, 1931
Lucas, F. L., Introduction to *The Complete Works of John Webster,* Boston,
Houghton Mifflin, 1928
Luccock, Halford E., *American Mirror,* New York, Macmillan, 1940
Millett, Fred B., *Contemporary American Authors,* New York, Harcourt Brace, 1940
Myers, Walter L., *The Later Realism,* Chicago, University of Chicago Press, 1927
Rovere, Richard, Introduction to *Light in August* by William Faulkner, New York,
Modern Library, 1950

Snell, George, *The Shapers of American Fiction 1798-1947,* New York, E. P. Dutton, 1947

Stravinsky, Igor, *The Poetics of Music,* translated by Arthur Knodel and Ingolf Dalil, Cambridge, Harvard University Press, 1947

Trilling, Lionel, *"Manners, Morals, and the Novel,"* in William Van O'Connor, ed., *Forms of Modern Fiction,* Minneapolis, University of Minnesota Press, 1948

Warren, Robert Penn, "William Faulkner," in William Van O'Connor, ed., *Forms of Modern Fiction,* Minneapolis, University of Minnesota Press, 1948

Wilson, Edmund, *Classics and Commercials,* New York, Farrar Straus, 1950

Periodicals and Newspapers

Birney, Earle, "The Two William Faulkners," *Canadian Forum,* June, 1938, 18: 84,85

Campbell, Harry M., "Experiment and Achievement," *Sewanee Review,* July, 1943, 51:305-320

Cowley, Malcolm, "William Faulkner's Legend of the South," *Sewanee Review,* July, 1945, 53:343-361

Faulkner, William, "An Author's Adjuration," *Christian Science Monitor,* October 4, 1951, vol. 43, no. 263, p. 11

Faulkner, William, Stockholm speech, *Saturday Review of Literature,* Feb. 3, 1951, 34:4

"General Introduction," *Faulkner Studies,* Spring 1952, 1:1-3

Howe, Irving, "The Southern Myth and William Faulkner," *American Quarterly* Winter 1951, 3:357-362

Jones, Howard Mumford, "Patterns of Writing and the Middle Class," *American Literature,* May 1951, 23:293-301

Minot, George E., Review of *Requiem for a Nun, Boston Sunday Herald,* Sept. 30, 1951, vol. 211, Section 3, p. 4

Starke, Aubrey, "An American Comedy," *Colophon,* 1934, Part 19

"Sweden's Nobel Prize Awards," *Time,* Nov. 20, 1950, 56:29

1 William Faulkner's Nobel prize speech, quoted by Bennett Cerf in "Trade Winds," *Saturday Review of Literature*, Feb. 3, 1951, p. 4.
2 "Sweden's Nobel Prize Awards," *Time*, Nov. 20, 1950, p. 29.
3 Bernard DeVoto, *The World of Fiction* (Boston, 1950), p. 43.
4 Alfred Kazin, *On Native Grounds* (New York, 1942), p. 461.
5 William Faulkner, "An Author's Adjuration," quoted in *The Christian Science Monitor*, Oct. 4, 1951, p. 11.
6 George Snell, *The Shapers of American Fiction* (New York, 1947), p. 89.
7 William Faulkner, introduction to *Sanctuary* (Modern Library edition, New York, 1931), p. viii.
8 DeVoto, *World of Fiction*, p. 43.
9 Lionel Trilling, "Manners, Morals, and the Novel" in William Van O'Connor, ed., *Forms of Modern Fiction* (Minneapolis, 1948), p. 149.
10 *Ibid.*, p. 160.
11 *Ibid.*, p. 160.
12 Joseph Warren Beach, *American Fiction* (New York, 1941), p. 4.
13 Elizabeth Drew, *The Modern Novel* (New York, 1926), p. 35.
14 Harry Hartwick, *The Foreground of American Fiction* (New York, 1934), p. 162.
15 Maxwell Geismar, *Writers in Crisis* (Boston, 1942), p. 148.
16 Harry M. Campbell, "Experiment and Achievement," *Sewanee Review*, July 1943, 51:306.
17 Malcolm Cowley, "William Faulkner's Legend of the South," *Sewanee Review*, July 1945, 53:360.
18 Earle Birney, "The Two William Faulkners," *Canadian Forum*, July 1938, 18:84.
19 Kazin, *On Native Grounds*, p. 460.
20 *Ibid.*, p. 460.
21 *Ibid.*, p. 460.
22 Geismar, *Writers in Crisis*, p. 181.
23 Beach, *American Fiction*, p. 148.
24 Kazin, *On Native Grounds*, p. 459.
25 Drew, *The Modern Novel*, p. 48.
26 DeVoto, *The World of Fiction*, p. 65.
27 Percy Lubbock, *The Craft of Fiction*, (New York, 1931), p. 116.
28 *Ibid.*, p. 116.
29 Lubbock, *The Craft of Fiction*, p. 185.
30 *Ibid.*, p. 144.
31 William Faulkner, *Intruder in the Dust* (New York, 1948), p. 209.
32 William Faulkner, "The Bear," *The Portable Faulkner* (New York, 1951), p. 243.
33 William Faulkner, *Absalom, Absalom!* (New York, 1951), p. 89.
34 Snell, *The Shapers of American Fiction*, p. 94.
35 Linn and Taylor, *A Foreword to Fiction* (New York, 1935), p. 104.
36 Fred B. Millett, *Contemporary American Authors* (New York, 1940), p. 34.
37 Richard Rovere, Introduction to *Light in August* (New York, 1950), p. vi.
38 DeVoto, *The World of Fiction*, p. 160.
39 Drew, *The Modern Novel*, p. 44.
40 Beach, *American Fiction*, p. 123.
41 Halford Luccock, *American Mirror* (New York, 1940), p. 48.
42 Geismar, *Writers in Crisis*, p. 167.
43 *Ibid.*, p. 167.
44 Snell, *Shapers of American Fiction*, p. 91.
45 Kazin, *On Native Grounds*, p. 460.
46 William Faulkner, legend of map used as endpaper, *Absalom, Absalom!*
47 Malcolm Cowley, introduction to *The Portable Faulkner*, p. 5.
48 Robert Penn Warren, "William Faulkner," in William Van O'Connor, ed., *Forms of Modern Fiction* (Minneapolis, 1948), p. 126.

49 Faulkner, *Intruder in the Dust,* p. 206.
50 Kazin, *On Native Grounds,* p. ix.
51 Drew, *The Modern Novel,* p. 143.
52 Trilling, "Manners, Morals, and the Novel," p. 153.
53 *Ibid.,* p. 154.
54 Walter L. Myers, *The Later Realism* (Chicago, 1927), p. 80.
55 *Ibid.,* p. 81.
56 Myers, *The Later Realism,* p. 19.
57 Faulkner, "The Bear," p. 291.
58 Faulkner, *Absalom, Absalom!,* p. 260.
59 Warren, "William Faulkner," p. 129.
60 Snell, *Shapers of American Fiction,* p. 88.
61 Malcolm Cowley, introduction to *The Portable Faulkner* (New York, 1951), p. 2.
62 Faulkner, *Absalom, Absalom!* p. 349.
63 Cowley, "William Faulkner's Legend of the South," p. 344.
64 Drew, *The Modern Novel,* p. 16.
65 DeVoto, *The World of Fiction,* p. 191.
66 Drew, *The Modern Novel,* p. 17.
67 Samuel Johnson, quoted in Drew, *The Modern Novel,* p. 253.
68 Henry James, *The Art of Fiction,* (New York, 1948), p. 22.
69 Drew, *The Modern Novel,* p. 71.
70 Maxwell Geismar, *Writers in Crisis,* p. 175.
71 William Faulkner, *As I Lay Dying* (New York, 1946), p. 397.
72 William Faulkner, *Go Down, Moses* (New York, 1942), p. 137.
73 William Faulkner, *Light in August* (New York, 1950), p. 48.
74 Faulkner, *Go Down, Moses,* pp. 111-114.
75 William Faulkner, *Sartoris* (New York, 1951), p. 280.
76 Birney, "The Two William Faulkners," p. 84.
77 Warren, "William Faulkner," p. 135.
78 Snell, *Shapers of American Fiction,* p. 91.
79 William Faulkner, *Sartoris,* p. 278.
80 William Faulkner, *Sartoris,* p. 287.
81 Faulkner, *Intruder in the Dust,* p. 245.
82 Drew, *The Modern Novel,* p. 121.
83 *Ibid.,* p. 125.
84 *Ibid.,* p. 125.
85 *Ibid.,* p. 125.
86 *Ibid.,* p. 125.
87 Faulkner, *Go Down, Moses,* p. 177.
88 Warren, "William Faulkner," p. 132.
89 see p. 34.
90 Warren, "William Faulkner," p. 134.
91 Faulkner, *Go Down, Moses,* p. 364.
92 William Faulkner, *The Hamlet* (New York, 1940), p. 196.
93 Hartwick, *The Foreground of American Fiction,* p. 165.
94 Millett, *Contemporary American Authors,* p. 96.
95 Luccock, *American Mirror,* p. 71.
96 Geismar, *Writers in Crisis,* p. 182.
97 "General Introduction," *Faulkner Studies,* Spring 1952, 1:2.
98 see p. 2.
99 see p. 3.
100 Faulkner, *Intruder in the Dust,* p. 202.
101 Faulkner, *Sartoris,* p. 347.
102 William Faulkner, *Soldiers' Pay* (New York, 1926), p. 317.
103 Faulkner, *Go Down, Moses,* p. 186.

104 Faulkner, *The Wild Palms* (New York, 1948), p. 156.
105 Faulkner, *The Sound and the Fury* (New York, 1946), pp. 308-313.
106 Faulkner, *Soldiers' Pay*, p. 319.
107 Harvey Breit, introduction to *Absalom, Absalom!*, p. v.
108 Kazin, *On Native Grounds*, p. 460.
109 William Faulkner, *Light in August*, p. 27.
110 William Faulkner, *The Hamlet*, p. 10.
111 Faulkner, *The Hamlet*, p. 58.
112 William Faulkner, *Collected Stories* (New York, 1950), p. 290.
113 Faulkner, *Absalom, Absalom!*, p. 35.
114 William Faulkner, *Requiem for a Nun* (New York, 1951), p. 38.
115 Campbell, *Sewanee Review*, p. 319.
116 Faulkner, *Sartoris*, p. 38.
117 Cowley, *Sewanee Review*, p. 354.
118 Warren, *William Faulkner*, p. 139.
119 Geismar, *Writers in Crisis*, p. 179.
120 Faulkner, *Requiem for a Nun*, p. 191.
121 Faulkner, *Intruder in the Dust*, p. 204.
122 Faulkner, *Collected Stories*, p. 669.
123 Faulkner, *Go Down, Moses*, p. 130.
124 William Faulkner, *Mosquitoes* (New York, 1927), p. 11.
125 Faulkner, dedication of *Go Down, Moses*.
126 Faulkner, *Intruder in the Dust*, p. 123.
127 Faulkner, "The Bear," p. 246.
128 Faulkner, *The Hamlet*, p. 43.
129 Faulkner, *Sartoris*, p. 35.
130 Edmund Wilson, *Classics and Commercials* (New York, 1950), p. 464.
131 Faulkner, *Requiem for a Nun*, p. 40.
132 Beach, *American Fiction*, p. 124.
133 Lubbock, *The Craft of Fiction*, p. 234.
134 Beach, *American Fiction*, p. 163.
135 Faulkner, *Intruder in the Dust*, p. 76.
136 *Ibid.*, p. 87.
137 Faulkner, *Intruder in the Dust*, p. 50.
138 Snell, *The Shapers of American Fiction*, p. 96.
139 Harvey Breit, introduction to *Absalom, Absalom!*, p. v.
140 Beach, *American Fiction*, p. 157.
141 Irving Howe, "The Southern Myth and William Faulkner," *American Quarterly*,
       Winter 1951, 3:360.
142 Kazin, *On Native Grounds*, p. 462.
143 George E. Minot, review of *Requiem for a Nun*, *Boston Sunday Herald*, Sept. 30,
       1951, sec. 3, p. 4.
144 Igor Stravinsky, *The Poetics of Music* (Cambridge, 1947), p. 65.
145 William Faulker, *The Sound and the Fury*, p. 314.
146 William Faulkner, *Requiem for a Nun*, p. 31.
147 William Faulkner, "The Bear," pp. 290-341.
148 Faulkner, "The Bear," p. 332.
149 *Ibid.*, pp. 295-315.
150 Cowley, *Sewanee Review*, p. 343.
151 Breit, introduction to *Absalom, Absalom!*, p. v.
152 Beach, *American Fiction*, p. 148.
153 *Ibid.*, p. 148; Wilson, *Classics and Commercials*, p. 463.
154 Beach, *American Fiction*, p. 148.
155 Linn and Taylor, *A Foreword to Fiction*, p. 26.
156 Campbell, *Sewanee Review*, p. 310.

157 Beach, *American Fiction*, p. 155.
158 Faulkner, *Absalom, Absalom!*, p. 86.
159 Faulkner, *Requiem for a Nun*, p. 18.
160 William Faulkner, *Intruder in the Dust*, p. 11.
161 Faulkner, *"The Bear,"* p. 262.
162 Lubbock, *The Craft of Fiction*, p. 71.
163 *Ibid.*, p. 111.
164 *Ibid.*, p. 71.
165 *Ibid.*, pp. 112, 113.
166 Lubbock, *The Craft of Fiction*, pp. 200, 201.
167 *Ibid.*, p. 211.
168 *Ibid.*, p. 255.
169 William Faulkner, *The Sound and the Fury*, p. 191.
170 William Faulkner, *Absalom, Absalom!*, p. 11.
171 William Faulkner, *Intruder in the Dust*, p. 93.
172 William Faulkner, *Sartoris*, p. 64.
173 Faulkner, *Sartoris*, p. 320.
174 Conrad Aiken, "William Faulkner: The Novel as Form," in Hoffman and Vickery, ed., *William Faulkner, Two Decades of Criticism* (East Lansing, 1951), p. 139.
175 Aiken, "William Faulkner: The Novel as Form," p. 140.
176 *Ibid.*, p. 142.
177 F. L. Lucas, introduction to *The Complete Works of John Webster*, (Boston, 1928), p. 16.
178 Warren, "William Faulkner," p. 143.
179 Geismar, *Writers in Crisis*, p. 145.
180 Drew, *The Modern Novel*, p. 17.
181 *Ibid.*, p. 17.
182 Andre Gide, *Imaginary Interviews* (New York, 1944), p. 141.
183 Howard Mumford Jones, "Patterns of Writing and the Middle Class," *American Literature*, May 1951, 23:299.
184 Cowley, introduction to *The Portable Faulkner*, p. 2.
185 Hartwick, *The Foreground of American Fiction*, p. 164.
186 *Ibid.*, p. 43.
187 Maxwell Geismar, "A Cycle of Fiction," in Spiller's *Literary History of the United States*, (New York, 1948), p. 1297.
188 Geismar, *Writers in Crisis*, p. 148.
189 Snell, *The Shapers of American Fiction*, p. 32.
190 Beach, *American Fiction*, pp. 161, 163.
191 Wilson, *Classics and Commercials*, p. 463.
192 Breit, introduction to *Absalom, Absalom!*, p. v.
193 Aubrey Starke, "An American Comedy," *Colophon*, 1934, Part 19.
194 Joseph Conrad, Preface to *The Nigger of the "Narcissus"* (New York, 1947).